ELEGIES IN
blue

Poems Benjamin Alire Sáenz

Cinco Puntos Press
El Paso•Texas

Elegies in Blue: Poems
Copyright © 2002 by Benjamin Alire Sáenz.

Acknowledgements

"Why Men Quit, An Intellectual Inquiry" appeared in *Chelsea* 70/71; "The Word 'Transvestite' Will Not Appear in This Poem" is part of a collaborative piece that accompanied the photographs of James Drake and first appeared in *Que Linda La Brisa* published by the University of Washington Press; "Work," and "Angel" first appeared in *Tex!*; "Elegy Written on a Blue Gravestone" first appeared in *American Diaspora: Poetry of Exile* published by the University of Iowa Press; "After Spain," and "What Was it All For, Anyway, Cesar, Cesar Chavez?" first appeared in *The Blue Mesa Review*.

Printed in the United States.

First Edition

10 9 8 7 6 5 4 3 2 1

NATIONAL ENDOWMENT FOR THE

ARTS

Funded in part by the National Endowment for the Arts

Library of Congress Cataloging-in-Publication Data

Saenz, Benjamin Alire.
    Elegies in blue : poems / by Benjamin Alire Saenz.-- 1st ed.
       p. cm.
    ISBN 0-938317-64-4
    1. Mexican-American Border Region--Poetry. 2. Mexican Americans--Poetry.   I. Title.
    PS3569.A27 E44 2002
    811'.54--dc21

                                        2001006843

Book and cover design by Antonio Castro
Cover photograph, "Light Haunting the Doorway" © 2000 by James Drake, taken at Rio Vista Farm in the Lower Valley of El Paso County (see page 117 for more about Rio Vista Farm). Section breaks within the book are taken from that photo.

Other books by Benjamin Alire Sáenz from Cinco Puntos Press are:
  • *Dark and Perfect Angels, A Collection of Poems*. Winner of a Southwest Book Award.
  • *A Gift from Papá Diego / Un Regalo de Papá Diego*.
  • *Grandma Fina and Her Wonderful Umbrellas / La Abuelita Fina y Sus Sombrillas Maravillosas*. Best Children's Book, 2000, Texas Institute of Letters

Contents

In Memoriam

Denise Levertov
José Antonio Burciaga
Arturo Islas

every writer should have such mentors

And always for Patricia, the woman
who has become my road, my map, my west, my south,
my way home

We are trying to retell history as seen from below. We do not talk over society's head; we do not speak as conquerors of History; rather, in keeping with the nature of our profession, we are notoriously on the side of the losers . . .

— Günter Grass

I.

Learning To Do
Philosophy

Oración: A Man at Prayer

I am here, amor, in the easy calm of a quiet

Room, alone, but the world is close, impossible

To banish. My desk is crowded with the unfinished

Business of living—papers, letters, postcards

I keep as if they were necessary as blood or bone

Or flesh. A candle with the image of the Sacred Heart

Is burning slowly toward its end. For now the flame

Is calm as this November night, full as an August

Moon, soft as your voice when you whisper, "te adoro."

The room is as warm as your hand the first time I

Touched you that summer afternoon. I am sitting here,

Amor. I want to run, stare into your face, make sure

Your eyes are black as I remember. That black has

Blazed with anger. That black is ash. That black

Is sorrow. That black is a room of forgiveness.

Amor, I am no longer a child. I have learned how

To speak in the hard language of the world—I want

My words soft as a new and tender leaf. I want to say

This: love makes nothing easy. The rich still imagine

Themselves to be kind and good and just. The night

Is still cold and many will not survive to see

The day. Love will not erase the poor, will do

Nothing to ease the hunger of the earth. A thousand

Acts of rage will fill the earth tonight. Love?

Love is something we suffer. Love is something we

Die of. And I am sitting here. And my candle of

The Sacred Heart is still warm from its own burning.

Tomorrow, this candle will give no light. I am

Afraid of the dark.

Amor, love is a weight, a burning, a long walk

Where legs and hearts grow tired. We never arrive

At the banquet. We have never been farther away

From the garden. But, amor, we keep walking. Come.

The night is long. Amor, I am calling your

Name. I am shouting it. Winter is coming, is here.

I am not afraid of the new season. The snow will

Melt. We will drink the new water. Amor, do you hear

My voice as you look out into the swallowing sky?

It is not God who calls. It is only me.

The Boy Learns to Ask Important Questions

The statues (antique and carved in a forgotten
Mexico); the altar (brought stone by stone across
The seas from Spain); leaded windows filtering
The Sunday flood of light (fire from the distant
Eyes of God). These are things that left the boy
Astonished.

Each icon in the church
Scrutinized like bugs and insects, plants and fruits,
And trees—the strange (but somehow common) things he
Found like a mad and crazed explorer on his father's
Farm. But insects, trees and crops were things that he
Could fathom. You could touch and smell—and know.
A carrot was a carrot; a worm, a worm. There was no mystery
To their purpose. What you did with a peach when it was
Ripe? The answer was: you ate it. What did you do with
A chicken? You stole its eggs—and ate them. And later,
Like the peaches and the eggs, you ate the chicken, too.
The rural life no mystery to the boy.   But
Statues and the altar and the portraits in the glass—
They pulled him by the collar (sometimes gently, sometimes
Not), their hot breath on his face, they called and called
His name. They held his heart, and held the story of
The world. They held the answers to each and every
Question in his head: What was the Immaculate Conception?
Who was Mary Magdalene and what exactly was a prostitute?

Why did the heart of Jesus burn but never catch on fire?
Were the wings of angels made of feathers? Did
The dying birds gladly give them up as they took their
Final breaths? And what was the stigmata? Did the wounds
Bleed and hurt forever? Was it something worthy? Was it
Something he should pray for?

❖

The words his parents used
Did not interest him: fertilizer, algodón, herramienta.
Carburetor, soil, irrigation. But there were other words
That made the boy's heart skip like a rock across a river.
The boy made lists of words he did not know, words he had not
Mastered, could not spell. He made a vow that he would
Learn them, learn them all before he died: covet, adultery,
Salvation. Annunciation, incarnation, beatific
Vision. Judgement, atonement, abyss. Genesis, mortal,
The eschaton. So many words he did not understand. Before he
Died, he'd learn and be the words.

❖

But there were other things he ached
To learn. His heart became a field of yellow grass that
Burned and burned in his unquiet mind as he drifted off
To sleep: Who was it carved the statues of the saints? Who
Made the colors on the windows that he loved? Who built

The church? Men or God or Angels? A thousand things he did
Not, did not know. Like the ripe and unnamed fruit on
Adam's tree. He heard a voice, perhaps a sainted serpent
Whispering his name: Pick. Taste. Eat. Waiting, calling,
Calling. Taste. Come and taste the sweetness. Then
Kneel in gratitude.

The Rags of Time on Río Vista Farm
(or A Short History of Clothes)

———

Then, the eyes of Adam and Eve were opened,
and they knew that they were naked; and
they sewed fig leaves together and made
themselves aprons.

—*Genesis 3:7*

I. Pentimento

I wander the grounds of this decaying

earth. Like a historian. I am not

another tourist. But what is

a historian if not a tourist who gathers

graves and facts and orders them. God.

The seduction of order. Better

to be a photographer. Better to be

a tourist.

❖

Once, the rooms

of this farm held children of the poor,

cradled them to sleep. Every night

for years, this place was like

a rocking chair. Beans and lullabies

to comfort orphans' tears. The beds were

free, the winters cold, the blankets thin.

Most days were Lent, though children

dreamt of spring and colored eggs.

❖

Then came prisoners
of war. They dreamt of home and rain
in Japanese. They cursed the drought and
cursed the cotton that they picked to pass
the time. Foreign, cruel, this cotton
thriving green in sandy soil—it made
them ache for touch, for wives and new
born boys they'd left behind. To touch
that kind of soft again. What war was
worth this price? To die? To die so far
from rain?

❖

All wars end. Even this, the worst of them.
Hitler dead. Japan brought to its knees. All
wars end. But there were other uses for this
farm. Braceros came with different
prayers on their lips. Mexicanos by
the hundreds, by the thousands, their
Spanish flooding empty rooms like water
floods the fields in early spring. Their
talk like candy falling from piñatas, full
of work, full of talk of money to be made.
Work. To work. *Arbeit macht Freiheit.* They came

with dreams, came because they dreamed.
We brought them for their backs, their
arms, their eagerness to work. Then hated
them, and put up signs to keep them
out of places where we dined. Come
work. Too bad you have to eat.

❖

Unburied bones, these empty buildings, left
exposed to rot. Scratch the surface
of this canvas, find a painting underneath.

II. Fashions

Socks and slacks, skirts and shirts. Dresses,
blouses, gowns. Ties, suspenders, hats and coats
and nylons bought on sale. Panties, bras
and cotton briefs. From seeds to plants to men
and women picking balls of white on warm October
days—from that to women weaving cloth. From that
to clothes and then to stores and then to bodies
walking down the street. And turning heads
that whisper words of envy. I love that shirt!
I wonder where she went to buy that skirt.

❖

"You look a million bucks! That dress!"
"What? This old thing? A rag, that's all. A rag."

❖

How many suits does a rich man buy
in a decade? How many pairs of slacks? How
many dresses for his wife? For the sons
and daughters sent away to school?

Weddings. Funerals. Graduations.
Parties. Birthdays. First Communions.
Winter. Spring. Summer. Fall.
For every season, something new.

Clothes make the woman, make the man.

III. Shirts and the History of Work

Shirts and shirts hanging in my closet. On the tags,
there are stories waiting to be published. I begin
the work of translation: *100% cotton made in
Hong Kong over for care 100% silk made in China
dry clean only 100% cotton fabrique a Philippines
53% rayon 47% polyester made in Taiwan 52% cotton
48% polyester fabrique au Portugal 100% cotton hecho
en El Salvador see reverse for care made in
Tunisia 100% cotton care on reverse 100% rayon
hand wash cold made in U.S.A.*

Farmers, growing

seasons, crops, harvests, truckers, factories,

weavers, dyers, workers, salesclerks, buyers,

boutiques, malls, cars in parking lots

Summer sale! 50% off entire stock of men's shirts

The history of work *made in China dry clean*

only 100% cotton made in El Salvador.

IV. A Pile of Clothes

This abandoned place, a poor farm once.

The history here is nowhere in a book.

Look, see this building—here, this

is where they processed Braceros, and these

the cages where they kept rabbits, good food,

and here, dorms for families, and here, here,

the kitchen, and this building, gone now,

who knows, foundations tell us nothing 'cept

the size of rooms, and here, perhaps

the prisoners of war.

        Vandals have broken

the panes. Layers of dust, nothing left

to keep out storms. In one room, rotting

mattresses, and here, here, signs

of a past, more recent: a pile of rotting

clothes: shirts, pants, dresses, blouses,

shorts, skirts. This place, as good as any

12

to toss what we no longer wear.

A pile of clothes. Those who wore them once
are dead. This is the story of the world.

The Boy Wants to Know About Names

(Predictably) these are names they taught

Him at the grade school in his desert town:

George Washington, Betsy Ross, Jonathan Edwards,

John Quincy Adams, Thomas Jefferson, Abraham Lincoln,

Cotton Mather, Benjamin Franklin, Mary Rowlandson.

And so (predictably) he learned to worship them.

He understood, by then, the different kinds

Of saints. Some you worshipped in a school. You

Worshipped others in a church. The command a simple

One: that he kneel before the names. Good

Catholic that he was, the boy was good at kneeling.

❖

He heard somewhere (though not in class), perhaps a

Whisper in a bathroom or the streets: Un-American

Activities. He liked, he liked the sound of it,

Cacophonous, dangerous, unmelodic. Un-American.

Un-American. He repeated it long into the night until

The song swam in his throat graceful as a dolphin in

The sea. He discovered (no, not in class) that there'd

Once been a committee, alive in the year he'd

Taken his first breath. A time of calm and
Innocence they said—though he did not believe
That hating Mexicans or Blacks was innocent or
Calm. And this he knew because he was a Mexican
And there'd been posted signs, letters bold
And proud, defiant: No Negroes, Mexicans, or Dogs,
In the fifties, in the fifties that we mourn.

                              He heard
These fragments of abandoned history in mostly
Unread books. Sometimes on aging, angry lips.
He read and listened. Learned. He loved, he
Loved the books. And loved the lips. And learned
To love the learning.

                              ❖

                    One day he found
A weathered book and read and read and read: the naming
Of the names. Naming, naming. The ritual public
Shame. What happened? If they named you? You
Would lose the job you had, lose the house you owned,
Lose the life you built and earned and loved. He asked
About a name (he'd liked the sound of it): Dalton. Dalton
Trumbo. Trumbo. His teacher said his time was better spent
On asking better questions. "Better questions?" "About
Better, better people." "Better people? Beaver Cleaver?"
The teacher's anger did not scare him. I am a communist.

He longed to say it, sing it, yell it. I am Un-American.
And then he laughed because he knew that Un in Spanish
Could mean "one" as in one hell of an American "I am
Un American." He laughed and laughed at his bi-lingual
Joke.

He searched and found
A litany of names: Marx and Engels, Gramsci, Emma Goldman.
Malcolm, César. Sacco and Vanzetti. He found groups
That were subversive (and wrote the meaning of the word
In a notebook that he kept). I. W.W., S.D.S.,
Socialists, Anarchists, Black Panthers, Brown Berets.
And once, in class, wanting to be brave (and perhaps
Subversive, too) he raised his hand and asked about
The slaves. "Did they have names?" he asked.
"Did they have names?"

❖

There'd be no end to names. Names
And names like rows of planted crops. Names carved
Straight on granite, a stone as black and cold as starless,
Winter nights. One day he'd go and stare, the names, trace
His finger on The Wall, repeat the names aloud, the names! O
God, the names! He'd cry and curse his teachers, curse
And cry and curse again because they'd never
Taught him what it meant. If it was you. If the name on someone's
Lips belonged to you.

Philosophy: The Woman at the Bar

I.

If a tree falls in a forest and no one's there to hear--does it make a sound? When is a chair not a chair? The answer to question number one: if the falling tree does not affect a human being, what difference does it make? The answer to question number two: a chair is always a chair. The problems the mind conjures are not difficult to solve. Aquinas? Augustine? Hegel, Kant? Heidegger and Marx? Trust your instincts, man! Trust your mind, your thoughts, your own philosophy. Believe! Believe what you see.

II.

You see that woman sitting in the corner of the bar? She poses a different kind of problem. She is smoking a cigarette as if she is clinging to the fading memory of her dead mother. She could sit and smoke this cigarette forever. In grief, she's learned to pose.

Picture her in front of a mirror a few hours before her arrival. See her staring into her closet choosing the right color of dress. Something to match her mood, her dark skin, her black unblinking eyes. She sees the dress she wants, scans for matching shoes. Color is important. Gold or silver earrings? Gold. The night was made for gold. Picture her as she hides the imperfections on her face, an artist, her own skin, a canvas. Women are illusionists. She combs and combs her hair. Finally, she is perfect. She nods approval in the mirror like a singer hitting a high C and holding it long enough to make the world take notice. She is ready for anything the hopeful night will bring. Watch her as she steps outside and takes a careful breath. She takes a swallow of the city's air and drinks it in.

Do as she does: taste the city. But you prefer the common taste of beer. Watch her now. She has you mesmerized. You wonder if she's waiting for a lover, or a friend, or the husband who deserted her. You devise a story of how she's waiting for a man (a man like you), a man to look at her as if she were an undiscovered continent, a man who'll explore and conquer her, a man she could love more than the cigarette she holds between her lips—more than the memories she clings to like a dying leaf clutching a branch. A man who will save her from this ordinary life. You know her familiar story. She is a woman. She has a role to play. And though it is you who has invented her sad and listless life, you do not fault your own imagination for the days you think she leads. There is nothing new. Not here. Not for her. Not for you. The problem here is loneliness.

III.

Come the day, by chance (or by Victorian coincidence), you see the woman once again. She is walking—in a hurry—down Avenida Juárez. You note the way she moves. Her muscular calves, the stylized movement of her hips. The night before she was softness and grace, her silk dress begging you to touch. Last night she was a dream, a perfect story in your head. And she was yours. Today, the morning light reveals a shadow on her face. Her make-up's melted in the dawn. Now she needs a shave. And then you know.

IV.

When is a man no longer a man? A change of clothes. Make-up on the face. Lipstick. Hormones shifting like tectonic plates. The tone of a human voice, a change of key. A tenor? A soprano? A body changing in the night—then changing back. The natural world refuses to stand still.

V.

Tell yourself again: the problem here is simple loneliness. Convince yourself: a woman is always a woman. A chair is always a chair. History is everything you have been told it was. Things were better the way they used to be. A man is always a man. It was a woman you saw last night. Refute all other answers. Trust your eyes, your instincts. Trust your first impressions. Trust the safety of your mind. Believe what you were taught. This is how you've learned to do philosophy. Last night, the tree did not fall. You heard nothing. The tree did not fall.

Why Men Quit: An Intellectual Inquiry

I.

There were different theories as to why his father had quit drinking. Alcohol poisoning. That particular theory was set forth by an aunt as she talked to another aunt at a family gathering. "It was either die or quit drinking. Por años y años no pudo dejar ese maldito trago. Pero al fin the doctor told him que se iba morir. His skin was all blotches. Fear of dying—por eso dejó ese vicio tan odiado." So really, his aunt's theory focused in on two interrelated and compelling reasons: Alcohol poisoning coupled with fear of dying. As far as the boy was concerned, the case she laid out was absolutely convincing. Hadn't he seen the blotches on his father's skin first hand? Wasn't he a witness?

II.

There were, however, competing theories as to the reasons behind his father's abandonment of the one and only art in his life he'd ever perfected. One of his father's friends put forth his own theory in the following manner: "Your father is made of steel. He gathered all his strength. Okay, it took him thirty-five years pa' hacerlo, but it takes a long time for a man to gather all his strength. But he did it. Strong, your father. Muy hombre. Only men of steel can beat the demon in the bottle." The boy's older sister mistrusted that particular theory. "Macho bullshit," she said. "Mom's stronger than Dad any day of the week. She's stronger even when she's sleeping." His sister had a point, and it was all but impossible to disagree with her. Hadn't they all seen their mother in action? She'd even held a thief at bay with a hoe once, and threatened to cut him down like a weed. What his sister said was true enough. No doubt about it. Still, the boy couldn't help but feel there was an important truth to the theory his father's friend had proposed. After all, you couldn't quit drinking without having discipline. According to his grandfather, you couldn't do anything without discipline—and he trusted his grandfather completely on all matters. The boy knew there was no discipline without strength. So—despite the rhetorical exaggeration and his sister's astute objections—the boy could not discount his father's friend completely. He wanted to become a true intellectual, and no intellectual of any integrity ever dismissed a theory, however far fetched, without a thorough deconstruction and a careful analysis. It is the responsibility of the scholar to weigh all the evidence at his disposal.

III.

In the matter of his father's drinking, his mother was silent. So the boy never asked her for the true reason. And he knew, beyond all doubt, that she held the truth in her heart, but there was no unlocking that truth, and so, over the years, he developed a simple theory about her silence: why re-live the hell? It was enough to have survived it.

He never asked his brothers and sisters about what they knew or felt or believed or heard about his father's entry into the world of sobriety. But he kept his ears open—just in case someone came along and spilled everything out in a moment of passion. There were many such moments in his family, and he thought this was a good thing, though his older brother did not share his optimism. "Belonging to a family is messy and ugly and embarrassing." That's what his brother said, and he was always telling people that he was an orphan, and ungenerous as this fib was, it was an improvement over the mythology he'd created as a child: "I was immaculately conceived!" He liked to yell that as he paraded down the street. But his sister (not one to take kindly to being disowned) used to follow him yelling out even louder: "Conceived in sin! Conceived in sin!"

IV.

To get back to the subject of the boy's father's drying out: one summer night, the boy heard his older brother (the same one who claimed to be conceived without sin and later claimed to be an orphan) talking to his older sister (the same one who liked to yell, "Conceived in sin!"). And his older brother said: "He promised Grandma on her deathbed. She had him summoned, sent the men of the village to comb the bars and bring him to her. When they found him, the stench of alcohol seeping out of his pores like incense from a censer, he went along quietly to the hospital. And as he wept at the foot of her death bed, she made him vow to never let the contents of a bottle ever pass his lips again so help him God. And Dad threw himself on the floor, swearing never to touch another drop. "Never, I promise! Never!" "So help you God?" she asked. "So help me God," he said. But that was the year his older brother joined the Thespian Club. He delivered his lines altogether too deliberately. Like incense from a censer? Who'd ever trust a man who spoke like that? No, no, like any actor, he was too in love with his performance. More in love with words than with the truth. The speech that spilled from actor's tongues was even more suspicious than the lies of macho drunks. At least no one gave credibility to the talk of men in bars. Actors, on the other hand, were altogether too convincing. The boy rightfully kept his distance from his brother's practiced fiction that masqueraded as an oral history worthy of serious attention.

V.

Many years later, the boy, now a man, and older than his father had been when he'd quit the bottle, did some quitting of his own: He quit smoking (a habit that was not only a habit, but a passion—and not only a passion but a love). In the moments that he craved the taste of smoke in his mouth, on his tongue, in his lungs, he thought about the theories he'd once heard concerning his father's drinking as he was growing up. He decided his aunt, and his father's friend, and his brother—all of them, decided they'd all been wrong. Sincere perhaps. But wrong. Not unlike scientists and doctors and sure-footed detectives and over-trained intellectuals, they had overlooked the obvious. The boy, now a man, suddenly understood perfectly why his father had quit drinking. He had quit not for them, his children; he had quit not because he was strong or made of steel; he had not quit because of a promise he made to his dying suegra, saint that she was. He had not even quit because he was afraid of dying. The last thing addicts are afraid of is death.

This. This was the reason why his father finally left the liquor that he loved: one night, his wife had simply asked: Amor, por favor, te ruego. Leave the bottle, now. Amor, me estás matando. All those years, he'd never heard her desperate pleadings. But in that moment, in the stillness of the calm night, something made him stop and listen to her voice. And, like the miracle of rain in the longest of droughts, he opened himself like a thirsty earth—and drank her words. He heard. He heard her lovely and familiar voice. The girl, the girl he'd loved and married long ago. And so, in the morning, his father woke a sober man. He never touched another drop. Not a single drop. This, then, was the whole truth of the matter. The other theories, each with their own impeccable logic, were complete and utter nonsense. His father, the subject and source of countless narratives, had quit the bottle for the simplest of reasons: he loved his wife. He wanted to spend a lifetime loving her. The boy knew this now, was certain of it. The boy was a man now, and he knew things he hadn't known before. He'd come to know the power of a woman who whispered salvation into the ears of the man she loved. Deserving of her love or not. The man she loved. In the night. In the holy, holy, night.

The Man Meditates On Being Middle-Aged

On that dry (or was it raining?) August dawn

he slid out of his mother's womb

as if (already!) he was in a race (lungs

hungry and grasping for a piece of air as

if it were solid as a meatloaf), as if

already he was sliding across second

base with the umpire sneering: "Sorry,

chump, you're outta there!" Like

a hero in any good story, he arrived in

medias res, in the middle of the game,

the bottom of the fourth inning, the

fifth chapter of a novel where things

were just starting to take an interesting

turn. No, the day of his birth was no kind

of beginning. When his parents woke on

that late November morning, desire

and need pasted to their eyes and thirsty

skin, they made quiet love (not wanting

to wake the children), that, that was
the beginning. No. They had made love

a thousand other times, had perfected
the art of making love in less than

romantic rooms, had begun what
they had, long before they made love

that early dawn. He, their son, came
along in the middle (was the quintessential

middle child—the fourth of seven.
Not so many, seven. Enough to place

him in the middle). Right now, it is
the middle of the afternoon and he was

in the middle of something when he began
to write his autobiography. The phone rang,

right in the middle of a thought,
and he spoke to someone about a project

he is in the middle of. He has reached
middle age. Forty-five, is in the middle

of his life. It is now the end
of the century. But the world might

last another two million years, so
he is living in the middle of history.

❖

He woke up this morning, in the middle
of a dream. Tomorrow, he will pick up

the dream (like a common and familiar
and well-loved coffee mug), right

in the middle. He has long suspected there
was once a beginning, but they have lied

to him about it so much and so often that
it has become nothing more than a beautiful

and unfathomable fable. Now, myths of
beginnings are as useful as spare tires

to a man who's wrecked his car. And the end—
the end lies beyond his imagination. (He

confesses to himself that he was once obsessed
with theologies of destruction, but he has

long since abandoned such useless
speculations about the end of the world

leaving such matters in the hands of

misanthropic ministers with small-minded

theologies who make their living by

blatantly misreading the holy

bible). No. No beginnings and endings for

him. Not for him. No grand genealogies,

no theatrical apocalypses complete with

locusts and rivers running with blood.

There is calm now. There is the walking of

his dog in the mornings, the beauty of

his wife as she speaks of her day, the good

book he is in the middle of reading.

Middle age is good for something—he's

learned his limitations. The middle

is what he knows, what he lives, what he

loves. The middle is his home.

A home. He thought he'd never have one.

II.

Now, No One Knows

Why You Fought

The Word "Transvestite" Will Not Appear In This Poem

Prologue

In the aftermath of the fire, all that remained of the cathedral were the old, stone tow-ers, the spires of the poor, the ruins of another time. The altar: ash. The place where you knelt and begged the old god for salvation is no longer. What you see from the front is only a facade. Your tears are all that's left of the old dispensation. Enter and mourn for what has passed away.

I. A Three-Room House

In Juárez: In another country: In the shadow of the Cathedral of Nuestra Señora de Guadalupe: a three-room house. A living room leads to a kitchen. A kitchen leads into a bedroom. A floor plan common as a taco, common as a spring wind, common as serapes and piñatas. Walk out the door and spit— you'll hit the street. Another spit, you'll hit "la calle mariscal." Spit one more time and find your DNA en el país del norte where English is a god.

On peeling walls, the hanging masks of clowns who cry and laugh (and made of cheap and fragile porcelain). The clowns, protectors of this house. The plants are silk, the flowers made of plastic. The couch is second-hand. The walls are spare, but even here there's art: aside from clowns, there's angels, vir-gins, sacred hearts on fire, statues (mass-produced) and rosaries.

In Juárez, every house you enter, a museum.

II. A Leisure Afternoon

They gather, ten of them, sit and laugh like women at a tea. A leisure after-noon. They talk of men (the men they've had, the men they want, the men they've loved, the men they've cast aside). Me quería. Me quería amarrada. Me quería en la cocina. Ni que fuera mi mamá. They talk of clothes, and make-up and of shoes (and sometimes whisper things about each other). They talk police, and talk arrests, and talk of rape. They talk assaults. They talk of clients who bruise, who hit, who bite. They talk of rights. And then they talk of earrings bought on sale. Some look like men. Some look like boys. Some look like girls. Some look like women, old before their time.

I listen from the kitchen, and smile at a picture of the Pope. A candle's burning on a shelf. An altar to the only virgin in the house, the patron saint of queens. I watch Carina paint her nails. The polish glistens in the light. The image on a calendar: a horse without a saddle, without an owner on its back; water from a river; the light of afternoon on tender leaves. A scene from Adam's paradise. The candle flickers in the room.

The supernatural and the natural worlds collide.

III. The New Dispensation

Permit me some statistics: Two are in their thirties. The rest are under twenty-five. At nineteen, one is just a boy. Or just a girl. But then again, they're middle-aged. Many won't see fifty. Any night could be their last. In this small thing, you must believe the writer of this poem: If they go on with this addiction, some will die an ugly death. Bludgeoned in an alley. On the border, though we are used to death, we don't like to use the word, and when we do, we say it with respect. (It isn't true we're all in love with death.) Come. See. Bring your eyes and heart. Walk across the bridge. ¡México! Come see the paradise. ¡Bienvenido! Play dress-up for a night. Be really brave—and try it for a week.

They sit and pose, shy and quiet, speak their names and where they're from. They have statistics of their own: Carina who is Carlos. Or is it Carlos who's Carina? (–S)He's from Veracruz. Michelle is from

Parral (who was Martín Mendoza). José Luis is now Leandra (also born in Veracruz—and this, her house). Mayte, Laura, Daisy, Norma, Jacaranda (she's the matriarch at 36). Norma, Paulina (the only one from Juárez), Guadalupe. And the names their parents gave them as a gift: Oscar, Enrique, Domingo, Guada-lupe (two of them)—and Luis. Exiles from Durango and Parral, from Delicias and Torreon, from San Luis Potosí and from Jalisco. Young (wo)men born in backward, ancient towns. And now, they lie with men they hope to love. They lie beyond their fathers' strict imaginations—and lie beyond their fists. They lie beyond their mothers' lullabies.

They lie beyond what most men ever dream.

IV. Cigarettes and Curling Irons
and Marriage

Unlike the mothers they abandoned, no one's in the kitchen. In the living room, in the bedroom, they're searching for themselves in mirrors, making sure there's nothing on their persons that can trace them to the towns where they were raised. Curling hair and curling lashes, cursing, laughing, talking, the contents of their purses on the floor: base, mascara, lipsticks, pencils, rouge—everything our sisters dumped out on the table—except, of course, for tampons. Each of them retreats when no one else is looking. They share their cigarettes, and smoke and smoke and smoke. They wonder at each other's clothes, wonder where she bought the skirt or blouse, wonder where she stole it, and how much were the boots? In the bedroom, Mayte's on the bed, the red blanket the same color as the rosary hanging on the wall, the same color as Selena's lips. The dead Tejano queen looks down on all her followers. And here, she's still alive. These women resurrect her as they change. Who's got a light? They smoke. They smoke and smoke and smoke.

And someone says, "I'm married, did you know?"

33

V. Danger: Artists at Work

Legs. Hair. Nose. Chest. Nipples. Arms. Hips. Cheeks. Lips. Thighs. A waist. A look. We die what we were born. We have the features of proud ancestors long dead. Aztecs, Mayans, Toltecs, Tarahumaras. Why disrespect? A million years to shape and redefine. To make us what we are. Hands. Feet. There's a use and there's a reason for our bodies.

A dress and make-up changes what? Is this a politics? Is this a revolution—Bolsheviks in drag? A leg that's shaved? A breast that's false? Tape down a penis—it's still there. A mask's a mask—and nothing more. A mask can't hide the man. James and I, we watch. And watch. We watch as they "transform" themselves. Se transforman.

And transformation's something that we know— it's something we're addicted to. New haircuts, clothes, new cars. We spend our waking days becoming someone else. Someone smarter. Someone better. We were born to change. Change ourselves and change the tired earth. Think of the computer. Think the internet. Think Picasso. Think da Vinci, think of Galileo. Nature's fine and good. But what of art? Art transforms the world. But this? But this? We watch. And ask ourselves:

What boy, who's sane, would want to be a girl?

VI. Miss Texas in a Pick-up Truck

The autumn sun has set. The dim bulbs of this house, our only light. Our eyes adjust. They're almost ready now. Life begins at night. They hide to change into their evening clothes. They don't let us see. They're girls. We're boys. No peeking 'till we're done.

Some look like men in drag—they couldn't fool a drunk who lost his glasses in a fight. Some are plain, and some are overweight—same as any woman made of flesh. And some have learned their lessons well: any man would want to touch (or taste). The transformation's a success. They gather 'round and pose. For one last shot. The Rockettes all in line. Miss Texas. Miss Utah. Miss Atlantic City. Which raving beauty will be crowned? These jokes are theirs—not mine. One knows the tune to "Miss America"—then hums aloud. And then it's time. They're working girls. It's time to hit the streets.

We step outside the safety of this house. Through dark and narrow streets, we drive slowly toward the bar: A Gringo. A Chicano. And Mexicanas, well-dressed and in heels, who sit and pose in the cold bed of a Texas pick-up truck—their hair blowing in the breeze. Picture them with purses on their arms. Picture them with long, white gloves. Picture them waving. At you. We should be in a parade. Or in some artist's photograph. The world should see itself.

The world should see itself transformed.

VII. Sueños

These women dream of Jackie O. and Norma Jean. They dream Diana and Madonna—they dream the land that worshipped them. Like us, they love the glitter of their clothes. If they can't have their bodies or their lives, they'll take their tragedies. Like us, they love that, too. These girls were born to men who bent or broke their backs so they could eat. These girls, like them, were born to work—and so they do. But they prefer the beauty of their dreams. They dream tiaras. They dream of fair-skinned beauty queens. They dream a leisure life. They dream a man to love them, one with charm and class like Cary Grant. Or Richard Gere. We feed them celluloid and lies. They're hungry, so they feast. We hate them for their hunger; we hate them for the way they've learned to eat. These women dream. Why not admire them? It's dreams, we like to think, that make us gods. Without them, we despair. So let them dream. Of Richard Gere. Of Jackie O. And Norma Jean.

Except they're men and always will be men.
Except they're men and never will be men.

Work

for the workers in the Juárez maquilas

On the border, we live in a desert of translation.

Our words are difficult and dry. How do you say rain?

How do you say river? How do you say the sand on which I

Walk is thirsty as a white sun? How do you say I live

In Juárez? ¿Cómo se dice Vivo en El Paso?

                                              To live

Is to dream of the river. How can you live without

The river? How can you live without dreaming? To dream

Then to laugh. To live in houses made of harvests

And abundance—bread and wine, asadero y chorizo,

Corn and chile. To live in houses where each

Room is for resting, for reading. For remembering.

Vivir. And live not only to work, but to live with

Time enough to rest in longing arms of lovers, of

Husbands, of wives, to live with time enough

To speak with neighbors of things that matter:

Did the premature baby born to the woman down

The street survive the endless night? Did you

View Doña Elena's body at the funeral home? How

Did she look? Did they remember to put in her

Teeth? Were the flowers I sent displayed?

And as the neighbors answer our hungry questions, to

Have the time to listen well, and then stoop to help

Them cut the flowers in their gardens, blooming

With the labor of hands they have learned

To use with grace. Hands. We have no use for wings,

Do not envy angels. Hands. In Spanish: manos. We want

To live. To live with time enough to wonder at the great

Mysteries: why trees grow leaves, why stars light up

The skies. To live not only to work. To live with time

Enough to cook, to eat, sit, shoes off, sipping on coffee

Warm as the evening sun. Then listen to the strings

Of a guitar that plays outside the window

Softly as the whispers of the dead. The dead

We love. We want to live.

        But to live, we must work. That word,

Work. In Spanish, trabajo. That is another dream. Dream. In

Spanish, sueño. My grandfather lived believing that work

Was holy. For him, if a man was not a worker, then he was not

A man. I have no argument with my grandfather. He's ninety-six

Years old. That man has worked enough. For him, these are days

Of rest. But we, we are still struggling with that damned word

Work. I don't say work is killing us. I do say we want to

Live and we cannot live without work. Why then do you refuse

To pay us for our labor? The stars do not belong to the rich, do

Not belong to the managers of maquilas where we waste our bodies

Working. But they, they have the time to sit in awe

Of the quiet desert nights, listening to the chollas struggling

To bloom. And us? Listen, work is not what's killing

Us. Listen. It is not the work. But we cannot live on the crumbs

You pay us for our blessed labor. Sorry. This is inexact. I

Live on a border. I am attempting to translate the words

I have borrowed and stolen, words now imprisoned

Somewhere between my throat and the suffocating air.

                            I want to live. I want to open

My mouth and scream: Work! We are dying! Work!

I feel myself disintegrating, becoming nothing but

Pure rage. But rage is cheap and common as desert

Dirt. Rage turns into hate sure as rain

Turns the clay into mud. You think I want

To hate? You think I want to be mud? I only want

To breathe. I want to breathe. I want to listen

To my heart as it beats like a piece of music

In a silence that waits to be broken. I want

To breathe. How do you say that in any language?

After Spain: For Edwin Rolfe

. . . and always I think of my friend who amid
the apparition of bombs
saw on the lyric lake the single perfect swan.

He carried the black

night of Madrid everywhere, memorized

each star, slept under those immutable stones,

their luminous weight whispering his name

in that strange tongue, a Spanish that spoke

to him only of death.

                            Dreams

came to him: fragments, friends, bullets:

arms, legs, heads, voices ceasing in the middle

of a phrase. Night after night, the speechless

battle raged. He would wake to the darkness,

then wait   to ensure the sun

would come. Perhaps, in the quiet of the dawn

he thought he might hear his fallen comrades

in the songs of the lark, understand what once

they started to say, the words they began to utter

in Spain.

                  He wrote in his neat notebook:

"Men dying in battle speak after speech has failed."

After Spain he knew how poor he'd always be, how he

could never be sure of meaning, never believe

the inevitable words he uttered to friends when

they came calling his name. He breathed, yet knew

himself dead. He'd died in the battle for Spain

the same way workers died in factories or in fields,

not all at once, not whole, the machine sanding off

the flesh, the bone, the heart a little at a time,

their bodies ceasing to be

                    before they ever died.

                         After Spain

there were never enough blankets in his house.

The roof and walls could not keep out the wind,

the rain, the memory of blood running like the rivers

of the West. The morning breath of his century

was cold on his skin. He never felt safe and warm.

And that bastard Franco, the new landlord

of Lorca's bloody earth.

                    Returning to his country

in defeat, the crowds greeted him as if he were

a stranger. The streets of his homeland could spare

no words of love. There was no time for tears:

another war was raging. He was called to fight

again—his heart still beating in the fields of

the dead, but after Spain there was only

Spain. Who was Hitler? Who was Mussolini?

                         ❖

When I walked those peaceful roads, Franco was burning

in hell—graffiti sprouting like flowers after a long

dark winter. When I was there, the hills were green
again, the blood had dried, the forty seasons of rain
had rinsed away the dead.

                Still, I could hear
the screams, could see the burning sky. The earth is
still in mourning. A thousand summer winds will not
sweep away the scent of bodies left to rot in fields
where once, before a war, wild grasses grew amid
the blue and lyric lakes. The waters have been dirtied.
Now, we will have to wait a million years before
we can drink there again. The grandsons of my grandsons
will be dead before the perfect swan returns.

In Memory
of the Abraham Lincoln Brigade

What Was It All For, Anyway, César, César Chávez?

It was as if you were born already

Knowing you belonged to the kingdom

Of the working damned, the lost land

Of bent backs where short hoes and pesticides

Were worshipped, adored as if they were precious

Images of Nuestra Señora, Reina de Los Angeles.

César, genetic memory

Is fine (if you go in for that sort

Of thing. So California). But you never knew

When to quit, just never learned how to give up

The brittle bones of the dead. Like some obsessed

Archeologist, you were always digging up

Another anonymous worker: Gonzalez. Herrera.

García. Hernández. They only exist now as names

On hieroglyphics, untranslatable into pedestrian

English. And, César, they were all

The same, all from a tribe with a particular

Genealogy, all from a long line of drones

Bred for service, bodies destined for picking,

Bodies with instincts for bending.

Descartes' dictum did not apply.

Not to them. They were not meant for thinking.

They knew only the language of work. And they were

Lucky to have jobs, no? What did they have

Without the labor this fertile country gave?

                    They died

Of natural causes. You say they died of work.

But work *is* a natural cause, César. Even writers

Die of work. Work. I can hear you laughing.

Nothing personal, I know. Go ahead and

Laugh. And anyway, who taught you how to spell

The word injustice? People hate it when you use

A word like that. Such a big word, César.

Too big for you. You, who loved the fight, who

Shoved back when you were shoved, you, César,

Should have known better, should have used a more

Flattering strategy. You wore that word out *Injustice*.

It made you sound accusing and superior. Not smart,

César, people got nervous. People hated you

Because you spelled it out—one lettuce

At a time. You told them what it meant.

Literate people don't like to be corrected.

People like food, César. They don't want

To know where it comes from. Don't politicize

Picking seasons. Already, they've politicized

Sex and sexual attractions. And now our Food?

                    ❖

You. More popular in death than in life (though

Some confuse you with that other Latin fighter

Who fights opponents he can beat. There's a lesson

There, César). You. Large as the California sun.

In death. You. Heroes are better manipulated when

They no longer have a voice to intervene in

The making of their own mythologies. Listen, César,

People are lining up just to say they touched you,

Wiped the sweat off your brow in the days when you

Were battling Goliath with a sling. I was there. I

Marched with him. He was my hero—and the rest

Of us listen, nod seriously. Some of us even

Weep. The ritual is all such good theatre.

You're an icon, now,

Sabes? And nobody gives one damned minimum-wage

Dollar that you broke your fasts by going

To communion at your local Catholic Church.

The Body of Christ did not save your causes.

I have a picture.

Of you. I ripped it from a glossy, New York

Mag. The man who took it, more famous than you.

You don't look like a saint or a prophet. You

Look like an ordinary mestizo who is fashionably

Unfashionable. A star, César. Now, no one

Knows why you fought.

Angel

*for Patricia (and the children
forced to appear in her court)*

Lost. Again. I chase a piece of

Paper on my always cluttered desk. I reach, pick up

The waiting phone, the numbers like a cherished line

From a favorite poem or prayer. I hear your secretary's

Voice as I pronounce your name. She knows it's me, your

Husband (my voice as known to her as the neat and perfect

Files on her desk.) "She's in a hearing, Ben. I can pass

The Judge a note." "No, just tell her that—" My voice falls

Off as I hang up the phone. I know you're out of

Reach before I even call. I know you're working, know

You're sitting on the bench—another case, another

Sordid story of a child mangled like a car in a wreck.

How can you listen to these tales of fractured lives? Day

After day, you sit. You listen. Day after day, I call. You

Cannot speak to me. But I can't keep myself from calling. A habit

I can't break. I glare at the phone, then continue my search

For that misplaced piece of paper. Thrown away, I think.

Thrown away? Careless. I'm so careless.

                          I walk back to my desk. I sit

And stare at the twelve photographs of you I framed and keep

So I can see you when you're somewhere else. I study

All the poses. I decide which look you're wearing at this

Moment of the day. I see you, sitting on your judge's bench.

Your face lights up the room, eyes as dark and shiny as your

Robe. I picture you scolding an unprepared lawyer. I picture

You asking the hundred difficult questions that must be

Asked. Those marks—who put them there? Does this boy eat? You

Do not shrink from your task. You have long since ceased

To be afraid. I picture you speaking with a child who's

Lived a life of fear. Love is as foreign to him as London

Or Madrid. I can hear your voice as you speak, soft

As a cloud floating across a droughted desert sky. I picture

The child answering your questions. I picture your eyes as

You listen. You hide your grief and rage. Your dark eyes

Know: Children are not papers on a desk. You don't shuffle

Them. You don't file them. You don't throw them out. Your

Dark eyes know: A child is a miracle. How could the world

Not know this? But the world does not have your eyes. Blindness

The disease of the twentieth century.

                        And then I picture

You and your Gabriela (my Gabriela, too). I hear your voices

Filling up the house. Your dark daughter leans into your

Shoulder, *Mamá, Mamá*. I picture you saving her life. I

Picture you saving mine. Again, I stare at the twelve

Images of you, my wife, my wife, mi vida. My eyes fall on the

Image where you're smiling. Your black robe's turned to

White. A million children. Reaching out to touch.

Elegy for Burciaga

(Written in an undocumented language)

Oyes, Burciaga, fíjate que I was listening to 93.9 "La Caliente" and I thought of you. Porque las voces en ese radio station comienzan a decir algo en español and all of a sudden they're speaking in English and, hombre, que te cuento, dicen unas cosas that would drive any monolingual person to question the meaning of language. Tanto a los Gringos como a esos Mexicanos orgullosos que también nos odian because we're such pochos and have no real appreciation for the structure, beauty and grammatical nuances of the Spanish language. Nos tiran unas miradas como fueran balasos. So nice to be hated by both sides. Bueno, la Chicanada's used to this.

¿Y sabes qué? We may need papers to cross the river, but la cosa es que we don't need papers to talk. And that's a good thing, because if we needed papers to talk, the Migra would never give us those papers and the barrio would be as quiet as a twelfth century monastery which the gringos and the Republicans would like, because even though they love our food, chiles rellenos, enchiladas, arroz con pollo, they're not so sure about the people who make it. It's funny ¿verdad? They like to name streets in Spanish, "Vista del Sol" y "Calle de Sueños" y que sé yo—so the moral is, it's okay to have a Mexican surname if you're a street. But if you're a person, bueno, maybe that's not so okay. Pero, tu ya sabes estas cosas and you're resting now. You've earned your rest, I know. You were so tired before you left us. And I hate to bother you. Pero, hermano, your door was always open. And you and Cecilia, you were always muy listos para recibir a cualquiera que les caía alli en Casa Zapata. And I don't forget. Bueno, I lock myself out of the house, because I forget the keys, and I forget where I'm going sometimes when I'm driving down the freeway.

And I forget English Department meetings all the time. But, Burciaga, you—
you, I don't forget.

Oyes, when I get tired of listening to the tonterias on "La
Caliente," I listen to K–B–N–A, "Que Buena," and on that station they also like
to bathe in linguistic impurity. Code switching is a soap we use to clean our-
selves, sabes? I think there are monitors from the English Only movement all
over El Paso. They walk around taking notes. This town really pisses them off.
El gusto que me da. Que se vayan mucho a la you know where. Bueno, they
still think que somos medios rústicos—unless of course, we act exactly like
them, speak like them, vote like them—in which case we're suddenly consid-
ered civilized, upstanding citizens who've managed to overcome our gene
pool. When we toss out our icons and worship their gods, all of a sudden we're
evolved. Makes me want to run out and get a tattoo. Except I hate needles.
Anyway, I'm too old for body art.

Burciaga, we'll never be good enough. Or as you liked to put it, they
think we're una bola de pendejos o mas bien they are the broom and we are
the dirt on the floor. They keep sweeping us up, but we keep coming back
inside the house every time a good wind storm comes along. Somos tercos.
We keep coming back. Show me a locked door and I'll show you a Mexican
who can figure out a way to open the door. Imagination's on our side. ¡Que
barbaridad! Y aunque uno pasa unos corajes tremendos aqui en la frontera,
tambien pasamaos unas curadas chingonometricas. I mean, baby, the talk of the
border's the best. I want to die listening to all this. Lie down and die. I swear.
God. The talk of our people, it's like listening to the rain. You know it and I
know it, and the reason we know it is because we are both insanely and illog-
ically in love with mestizaje. Bueno, what can you expect? Somos hijos de la

conquista. Pero siquiera nunca fuimos agachados. Okay, so we're always fighting with the wrong ammunition. That doesn't mean we're not fighting—it just means we're not winning.

Mira, yo sé que tenías tus quejas con El Paso. Bueno, the whole world está en pleytos con esta ciudad tan dejada. Pero, we're still here. They call us dead—pero fíjate que no. After all the funerals, we're still here. Making tamales and eating menudo at two o'clock in the morning on Alameda at the Good Luck Café. Don't believe everything you read in the newspapers. We're still here, Tony, so put in a good word for us. Remember, you were ours from the very beginning. And you will always be ours. No se te olvide de nosotros. El Chuco loves you, baby.

Photograph: Fidel and Che, 1964

I.

Everything about them's so familiar.

Like Marilyn and J.F.K., we knew

Them once. Devils, Angels, Devils. Depends

On where you live. Depends on what you dream.

Angels then. A better world, they yelled—new

And equal, pure as Cuban rum, warm as

Caribbean rain. The old world order

Rotting like an over-ripe banana.

We're not a five-course meal for you to eat.

Leave! Go! Go find an Eden of your own.

Play at Vegas, Cannes, Atlantic City.

If only Marx had lived to see this day.

The message of these angels so familiar.

We loved them once. We'd know them anywhere.

II.

The older man, the one who's clung to life

Though now he's old and mean as spit some say—

Like the city where he lives. !Havana!

Havana de los sueños we misplaced.

He wears the same drab robes like a priest at

Daily Mass (A savior's work is never

Ever done). His face is framed by his green

Cap (the photo's black and white—but we fill
In the color). He remains here what he
Was: thin, agile, playful. The armies are
At rest. He basks in quiet now, a pure
And simple joy, he's lighting his cigar,

The smoke the center of all light, his face
An ember, burning, burning in the night.

III.

And seated close, a comrade. His wild hair
Unable to be tamed. He drapes his arm
Around his friend, Fidel. So calm, but not
At peace (not that). Even here, now, among
His intimates, he watches, watches, waits,
A sentry, cannot rest. We'll remember him
This way: militant, proud, impervious to
Bourgeois impressions. Unrepentant to
The last, stubborn and beautiful in ways
Men want to be—if only for a day.
If only for a blessed, blessed day.
The revolution's star. Not hard to guess

Why women loved. Not hard to see which one
Would bleed. Young. Die. Beneath an angry gun.

☑ The Stranger Goes Home

(For Jimmy Baldwin)

The world is white no longer,
and it will never be white again.

I don't remember when it was
I started reading you. By then
I was a man. Angry, the world
having caught up with me. No
longer able to pretend the rage
did not exist (sometimes, I could
feel its heat like a fire
blazing in the riot of my heart.
And in the cold, believe me, any
fire's home). It took me
years to understand the aesthetic
of an angry crowd, the logic
of its chaos. I never
recognized my own contorted
face, my own inhuman voice among
the shouting in the streets.
I was educated. I was civilized.
The price of the ticket did not
matter—I would have paid anything
to be loved by this America. I refused
my supporting role among the throngs
of perdition. I would have paid
anything. But you were right, Jimmy,

rage becomes a daily bread, sweet

as a communion wafer and almost

as holy. And one more thing: rage

can be silent as my Catholic

God.   Rage

can only with difficulty, and never

entirely, be brought under

the domination of the intelligence

and is therefore not susceptible

to any arguments whatever. And you

were right again: those who've never

felt the rage have small imaginations.

So here I am, so many years

later, a Chicano returning

from the desert picking up your

book (again) like I was picking

cotton—and learning late

to give the land that gave us

breath, the dreadful name it's earned.

❖

Rage is a hard companion.

It turns the heart to stone. Not yours.

Your heart was always flesh. But wounded,

too. I sometimes saw your bruises

on the page.   When

I was told, it takes time, when I was

young, I was being told it will take time
before a Black person can be treated
as a human being, but it will happen.
We will help to make it happen. We
promise you.

❖

I had a dream
of you: writing in your room. The room
is spare and it is blinding white.
That white is killing you. And isn't
that the way it always was? Por los
siglos de los siglos, isn't that
the way it will be always?

I see you spelling
Giovanni over and over, mistrusting
your own knowledge and intelligence, doubting
even your ability to spell—and in
those brutal seconds, succumbing
to despair.

❖

What has happened in the time of
my time, is the record of my ancestors. No
promise was kept with them, no promise

was kept with me, nor can I counsel
those coming after me, nor my global
kinsmen, to believe a word uttered by
my morally bankrupt and desperately
dishonest countrymen.   Jimmy
when you died, did you think of
Jesus? Did you recall your father's
God? Did he shout, reject, condemn?
Did he finally embrace? Did you fall
into his arms at last to rest? At last
to rest, the rage subsiding like
the waves of a slumbering sea. Did you
think: at last I'm free of having to
choose the perfect words, the right
tone of voice to make white men see
what they refuse to see. At last
free of the prison of words.

Home, Jimmy, the only heaven you
wanted. No longer a stranger.
The shouts of the village behind you.

American Camps

On the Inside Looking Out, Refugee Camp. That is what is written on the photo postcard, circa 1914. A crowd of Mexicans, unaware of the camera, is standing at the edge of the desert camp. Invented for cattle in the previous century, clever men found other uses for barbed wire. Later, this same invention will be used to encircle the Japanese and Jews. The Japanese. And Jews. But all of that is still a future dream. Here, in this photograph, it is still 1914, the fourth year of the Mexican Revolution. Three years to go. These things take time. But in this photograph, those it has captured in its gaze will never age. The men are in hats. The women in long skirts and rebozos to protect them from the sun. Or the cold. The sky, I imagine, was blue that day. And clear. Not unusual for El Paso. And a boy, not waist high to a grown man, flirts with the camera. There is genius in this face, this boy's expression, as if he knows what we can only guess. This many years later, in the safety of this library, I am left to wonder what became of this clearly intelligent boy. Did he have a good life? Was he finally broken by the cruelties of his circumstance? Did his brilliance survive the jealousies of his adopted homeland?

It is clear that the lens is sympathetic to the plight of this dark people who have fled the blood and betrayals of the revolution. They have left their homes with nothing. Their future lies in this alien land. They seek asylum. A worried resident (not pictured) does not share the camera's sympathies. They are aliens, civilians, indigent, unhygienic and liable to become public charges and in fact are obnoxious to every law governing the admission of aliens into the United States. Worse things than this were said. Various forms of name calling. Sticks and stones may break—you know that poem. The camera lies. They were not loved. I am telling you the truth. You can go to the photographs division of the Library of

Congress. Ask Them. They will show you the picture. Keep searching and you will find a record of the voices of the worried American citizens and what they thought. Comb through the stacks and search for obscure ethnic histories. Unread books in the Library of Congress—that's where history is hidden.

III.

Elegies in
Blue

The Blue I Loved

*Maria de Guadalupe Cenizeros, citizen of Smeltertown,
sings a lullaby explaining the color
of the headstone on her grave*

I loved the August rains, I loved the calm October

days. I loved the sound of thunder as it echoed

in the nights; I loved the breeze that made my curtains

dance a waltz. I loved the water in the river,

chocolate as my skin.

                   I loved the smell of beans,

the smoothness of the masa in my hands. I loved

the stacks of fresh tamales on the stove, the

taste of yerba buena on my tongue. I loved

the rows of chile in the fields.

                   I loved the look on Mama's face

before she closed her eyes and never woke again.

I loved the worn wood rosary she left to me, her

only child to live past thirty years. I loved the

picture of her wedding day. I placed it next to mine.

I looked like her. That is what I loved: I had her

face, her eyes.

                   I loved the stove where I cooked meals

as simple as the wood I walked on with bare feet.

I loved those pisos made of wood, and loved the Little

Flower of Jesus. She made me hers. And just like me

she loved the smell of candles and copal. I loved

the afternoons we talked, just she and I.

                                    I loved to wake

the house each dawn. I loved my children's grumbling

as they rose to meet the sun. I loved their look

of hunger as they ate. I loved their loving me.

I loved their look of pain when I grew sick.

Their tears burned like the sun the day I died.

                        I loved my husband's eyes. Green

as apples growing on a branch. I loved his

hand upon my back. The roughness made me tremble.

Forty years that man could make me tremble. He's

buried next to me. In death I swear he snores.

We sleep the way we lived: in peace. And one

more thing I loved. I loved, I loved the color

blue, the color of the room where we made

love and slept. Where we made love and slept.

I loved the color blue.

The Boy Falls in Love With Beginnings

Eschatology. The word rolled off his tongue and fell toward
Nothingness. He struggled with the spelling, writing several
Versions on the page. He guessed and guessed until he spelled it
Right, then looked it up: from an ancient word in Greek, eskhatos,
It said. Last. Extreme. The study of the ultimate: death
And judgment, rapture, heaven, hell. Omega day, the dying
Of the sun. A science? To know such things.

                                   It was then that he
Decided—that's what he'd become: an eschatologist. Much better
Than a doctor or a priest. That spring and summer, he read
The Book of Revelation, and pictured the destruction of the
World, the wild fires burning all the green, drying up the
Seas until no hint of paradise remained. It hurt his heart
To think about such things. His brothers, sisters, José and
Linda, Gloria, Jaime and Ricardo, they would all be lost,
Their bodies charred and lifeless. His cousins, uncles, aunts,
His friends at school. His Mom and Dad. The things he loved, dogs
And cats, bears and trees, rain and wind and snow. Cokes, pecans,
Chile, fruit, tortillas, beans, the soups his mother made
To warm him winter days. Their farm, the Rio Grande, the mountains,
And the desert and the blooming yuccas in the spring. All
Of this destroyed. The earth he loved and knew becoming nothing but
An urn for keeping ashes of the dead. What good was that? The end.
What good to study that?

One August night, he dreamed a sky, and it was burning

Blue. And when he woke, he knew it hadn't been the end. He turned

To reading Genesis. And fell in love again. With earth and reeds

And water, with birds and words and birth. He watched a baby

Learning how to walk, and watched him fall, then watched him rise

Again. He woke at dawn and watched his grandpa, old, the morning

Lighting up his face. "Smell," the old man said, "Hijo! Smell!

The earth is waking, darkness gone. Hijo de mis ojos! La luz de Dios!

You can smell the light."

"Denise Levertov, Poet and Political Activist, Dies at 74"

—

That was the headline

in the obits in

The New York Times. December.

A good month to die.

'97 was a warm winter

on the border. Was it cold

in Seattle?

It was night

when Rose called.

I couldn't talk.

I picked up your last

book. I held it

in my hands. I stared

at your poems. That night

they were just words.

Poetry can praise, can dispense

wisdom, can console. Denise,

there are times that

words are shallow—

to utter them is to

insult the dead. And

to insult the living, too.

I couldn't talk.

❖

I had a dream.   I heard a voice:

When you are hungry   that is when you know food.
When, you are thirsty   that is when you know water.
When you are dead   that is when you know death.

I woke and asked   When do you know God?

❖

Did poetry matter in the end?

❖

What was the last question you asked?

❖

You were older than my mother. I never
thought of you that way.

❖

I see you riding a bike.
I see you looking into my
face, explaining something
urgent. You are trying to make

me understand. You think
I am being stubborn. I think
you are being stubborn. I see
you climbing the steps to
your house. You are surrounded
by flowers. You know the name
of each of them, know which
seasons they will bloom. You turn
and point at a heron on the lake.
I am walking next to you
at a march. I turn and read
the sign you hold. The words
become a poem and you are
reading it. I see your hands
moving across the keys
of a piano. Never
enough music, books, rain.

❖

I don't remember if I thanked you
in the end. For what you gave.

❖

Denise, you who believed
in politics and art

and poetry and God,

you who became Catholic

in the end, tell me

that death is not

a bitter thing. There

has been enough loneliness

and rage in the living.

Tell me we are done with that.

Tell me the poor were saved.

Tell me the poor were saved.

The Man, Having Dreamed that He Died, Writes A Long-Winded Epitaph for Himself In the Third Person

—

At the time of his death, he was engaged

In a long-term political argument with

The country he inherited from his parents.

He preferred trees to nations—and never

Mistook America for paradise. He never tired

Of reminding anyone who'd listen that

"Under God" in the "Pledge of Allegiance"

Was not in the original, the unfortunate

Addition of a later redactor.

He was a practicing,

If unorthodox Catholic, and even confessed

His sins from time to time. When it was

Brought to his attention that he'd never once

Voted Republican, he was unrepentant. He was

An ex-priest, ex-smoker, loved wine, loved dogs,

Loved to grow tomatoes. He was the son

Of Juan Sáenz and Eloisa Alire. He treasured

The name they gave him till the last sweet

Breath he took. He was better at loving sisters

Than at loving brothers—and for this one sin,

He was heartily sorry.

He loved to read

A good poem, argue with a bad one—his own

Included. He loved, he loved to write.

Before he died, his books were out

Of print. He mourned their passing. But not

Much. He loved to study the various looks

On his wife's face—in this one thing

He claimed to be an expert. He had some

Enemies—well earned, he hoped. And had more

Friends than he deserved.

He loved to lie awake and listen

To a storm. And when it passed, he slept.

He loved November nights. Each spring

He turned the earth, and tried to coax

A crop. He loved a summer heat that turned

The blossoms into fruit. He was a farmer

In his heart. For his reward, he's now

Become the earth he loved to hoe.

I.

At the Grave of Karl Marx

You never saw this century,

but, God, you were alive! Alive,

Karl, in 1917. The workers

picked your words like ripe

apples. What a harvest it was!

You should've seen it. And

You lying here in England.

That's worse than being drunk.

God, Karl, England. That.

That was exile.

Worshipped and hated—like

Jesus, Karl. First, it was

God who was dead. And then

it was the age of industry

that took a dive toward

that inevitable end. Now,

it's you. Dead, Karl. The one

irrefutable dictum

of a materialist theory

is that we die. In time

we'll all be dead

as the Revolution. Dead

as demonstrations on May Day.
This year, Russia's workers
didn't march. No birds
in that nest this year.
And something else—
the Capitalist machine
is purring away in China
like a cat taking a nap
in the window of a suburban
house. Have you heard? Karl,
it's all gone. Dead, I
tell you. Dead as
the Romanovs. Dead as
your thoughts. Theories are
like people, Karl:
One dies every day.

But the news is not
all bad. Take heart. Students
are lining up to buy your
bible at second-hand bookstores
all over San Francisco.
Every day, someone resurrects
your words. And the young are
shouting in the streets
again. They shut down Seattle.
They're making noise
again. Theories are like people,
Karl. One is born every day.

At the Grave of J.F.K.

Forgive me. Not even the memory
of your widow's poise nor this
eternal flame can make me mourn.
Today, I haven't the stomach for
nostalgia. The truth about you is
as common as E. coli on hamburger. Listen,
Mexicans everywhere worshipped
you. We thought you loved us. Is
that your fault? That we believed?
Your photograph in every barrio house,
ubiquitous as statues of St. Joseph.
Such a handsome saint. I saw your
smile every day. Good teeth, Jack,
strong jaw.

        Mrs. Collins cried
her eyes out. "He's dead!" her grief
her trembling voice. "Shot! They killed
our President!" Fourth graders, we stood
straight in our rows and prayed
for you. We bowed our heads. We knelt.
Because you loved us.

Our teacher loved you more
than she loved us. I thought

she'd break. That's what
I remember. Our teacher loved

you more. When I came home, I found
my mother crying. Tears sprinkling
my father's shirt as she pressed it
with her iron. Crying, Jack, because
you loved us. I found my mother
crying. I don't forgive you.

(III.)

At the Grave of Pancho Villa

Child of the lower
class, peon, unschooled, former
outlaw, you had nothing in common
with Marx or Lenin. Nothing
in common with Fidel or Mao or Che.
Where was the theory, Villa? You
hardly had a politics at all. Except
you knew that Mexico belonged
to those who worked the land. The rich
you sent to hell where they belonged.
You loved that fight.

Escogiste un gran panteón en
tú Chihuahua. El hombre pone. Dios
Dispone. You hadn't planned on

resting in Parral. Bueno, there
are worse places to be buried.
Mexican earth is Mexican earth.

If you hadn't fallen in love
with cars, if you'd stayed
on your horse—then maybe you'd
have stayed alert, wouldn't have
let down your guard. Listen,
at least you were driving the car.
Almost like dying in the saddle.

When you heard that familiar
shout: "¡Viva Villa!" you didn't
expect a rain of bullets. Rumor
has it you died instantly. Nine
bullets to kill Villa! Nine! Those
pinchi assassins had no respect,
didn't bother to look you in
the eye before they took aim
and shot. And again the blood
flowed on the streets. Such a common
sight in this century of killing—
common as the people who fought
by your side. When you heard
the shots, you must have known.
Well, better bullets than cancer
for a General.

Next day, the blood
on your shirt still wet, they
buried you. They haggled over
the price of your embalming.
You! ¡Villa! They had their ways
of getting back at those who
didn't keep their place. Did
you think they'd ever love you?
Killing is the least of it.

❖

And, now, they've moved you
here, to rest en la capital,
largest city in the world.
Imagine! ¡Villa! Descansando
en paz en el Monumento de la
Revolución. Rest is not what
you wanted. Listen, Villa,

your people are still poor.
Villa, if you would rise
again. To fight. Millions
would still follow. Millions.
I thought you should know.

IV.

At the Grave of David Macias

This year, the heat came early.

I'm growing tomatoes again. Last

year, a blight, the crop was sad

and sparse. This year, I hope for

more abundance from the earth. Already

the signs are good. The grass

this spring is green. The cactus

gave us flowers, yellow as

a morning sun. The palo verde

in the front is still in bloom—

no heat can stop its limbs from

reaching toward the azure

of this ancient sky. Here,

the plants are like the people—

they refuse to die. The fight

is a beautiful thing. A few years

back, I planted a cholla

that's become a tree. It has no

need of water. It grows. And grows.

I love that stark and leafless tree.

And love your daughter, too. We bought

a house. Six years I've been

her husband. You should see what

she's become, a woman, unafraid of

this land or the harshness of the

sun, unafraid of the infernal winds,

the droughts, the days that test her

will. She has become the desert.

I wish you could come and make

a visit. I'd show you the house.

We could sit on the steps, drink

beer, eat. We could talk late

into the night and watch

the stars. You could tell me

about your life. I could tell you

about mine. I love your daughter.

I came to thank. To thank you, sir.

V.

At the Grave of Juan Lucero Sáenz

El Polvo, the place of your birth.

They've renamed it Redford. "Bueno,

los gringos cambian todo." Known, now

as the place where Ezequiel Hernández

was killed at eighteen by uniformed

patrols. Your land belongs

to soldiers, now. They mistook him

for the enemy, shot him like a deer

in hunting season. Sorry, they

said. A Mexican on the border?

A mistake? Maybe. Maybe not. He was

asking to be shot. "Querían más a los
perros que a los Mexicanos. Y todavía
no nos quieren."

We have always been the enemy.
You didn't hate them back.
You didn't waste your time.

❖

People crossing back and forth, a daily
ritual. Like morning Mass. In your
boyhood, the river was a river. Not
a border. I see you, a boy crossing
passengers on a raft for a penny. I see
you, a skinny youth, jumping trains
to Colorado. You became a man by building
Texas roads: I see your face, your steady
hands lighting dynamite, clearing
the path for those behind you. At my age,
you were mixing fuel for secret
launches at a missile base. You kept
your secrets well. Who would you tell
—you who spoke no English?
I dream you in a hat, standing
in your garden, grower of grapes, grower
of chile, grower of squash and corn.
I remember your hands on my shoes as

you tied them. I remember your laugh,

the way you said my name. I kept your

glasses, placed them on an altar

in my house. When I grow old, I want

to see. The world. The world you knew.

❖

Grandpo, you were sweet

as summer peaches. The earth was

all you had—and all you loved. You

took what it would give. Old and

spent, you are a river gone dry.

I will never drink there again.

IV.

At the Grave of the Twentieth Century

Let the dead bury the dead

Not that they buried you anywhere.

But if they'd thought enough

of you to lay you in the ground,

they might have buried you, here,

in El Paso/Juárez, dumping ground

of the Americas. Not that you

would have known any rest here.

Peace is not in great abundance

on the border.

❖

And what exactly would you
have liked as an epitaph? A photograph
perhaps, no imprecise words cluttering
up the simple granite stone. An image
of Ghandi, perhaps? Desmond Tutu?
Idi Amin? Hitler? Roosevelt? Truman
Capote? Elvis Presley? Rock Hudson?
Elizabeth Taylor in her prime?
Jackie O? (Was it really the American
Century?) Churchill? Thatcher?
Mandela? Mother Theresa? Elizabeth II?
Or her tragic nemesis, Diana?
Chairman Mao? The Emperor Hirohito?
Charlie Chaplin, Ronald Reagan?
General Patton, General Powell?
MacArthur, General Franco, General
Pinochet? Any General at all? Benito
Juárez? Zapata? Juan Perón? Evita?
John XXIII? Picasso? Yes, Picasso.
No, Andy Warhol? Perhaps a writer?
Octavio Paz? Neruda? Faulkner?
Pound? Garcia Marquez? Dorothy
Parker? Jacqueline Suzanne? No,
not a writer. A thinker? Yes?
Sartre? Foucault? Antonio Gramsci?
Malcom X? Franz Fanon?

❖

Let's scrap heroic

individuals. How about something more

communal, a group picture instead?

A sports team, perhaps? After all, when

was the last time there was a World

Cup without blood on the ground? What's

a Super Bowl without the aftermath

of a riot? There are more ways to

violence than we'd ever imagined.

Sports, the new opiate of the people.

Why not

keep it simple? Let's list the names

of those who died in wars. Too long

that list, you say? No wall could

hold the names. Let's skip the lists

and litanies. Let's etch into the stone,

these simple words of grief:

Here lies the century of death, the century

that taught us how to sing: "*Deutchland,*

Deutchland. . ." We looked upward

not to see a God or doves in flight

but to avert our frightened eyes.

You, the century that was our home,

that was our place of birth, you have become

idea, have become prologue, myth, have been passed from the working hands of soldiers, maids and janitors to the heads of white historians. Much will be written. The dead are already forgotten.

We miss what you gave. We are doing our best to bring you back to life. *"Deutchland, Deutchland, uber alles . . ."*

Elegy Written on a Blue Gravestone
(To You, the Archaeologist)

What history is:

a mound of gathered rocks. In time the rocks will

melt, will turn to dunes of sand, will blanket everything

you fought your wars to keep. All that work and worry;

the countless sleepless nights; the house you built

and loved (thirty years of paying right on time);

the perfect car that lasted forty years, the ring

you gave your wife, the clothes you bought your sons.

All buried now, those things (the worries, too).

Remember this: everything will die except the desert

sands. Everything will fade except the ashes of the

earth we filtered through a smelter's lonely tower.

The smelter, too, has died. And one day, soon, the tower

will be dust (not unlike your car; not unlike your

house; not unlike your wife). All debris and ashes.

❖

Pick up a spade. Roll up your sleeves

and dig. Wipe the sweat from your brow. Then dig deeper,

deeper still. You cannot stop. You're a worker now.

Pray to God to find the heart you lost here long ago.

You need it now. Pray. Dig. Laugh (if you can) at

the blatant irony: to end your days doing what you

hated. Fated to become an archaeologist.

❖

See this artifact? Laid with crude cement and painted
blue. Deep as moaning from a mourner. Deep as scars
on Jesus' arms and feet. A gravestone, a marker, not
granite, not marble, a common monument befitting
the class and taste of the deceased (or the survivors).
The inexpensive cross with corpus (bought retail
at a shut-down shop on Stanton Street). History
is buying and selling. History's an aisle of icons.
History's a birth, it's a funeral. History's a rose
made of plastic. History's a grave with no date.
History is broken cement. History's a litany
of questions: How many minds wasted at the plant?
How many bones fractured? Broken? Mended? How
many hearts shattered like a cheap ceramic cup?
Find the pieces, archeaologist! Reconstruct the
hearts! Remember this: these ruins guard their
solitude. They've fought their wars, and fight them
still. Ask anything you like.
You will not make them speak.

❖

A son or son-in-law, in grief,
designed this monument. A daughter picked the paint.
They thought their work would make the world remember.
There was a day: this painted blue cement was God
in heaven's envy. Not now. No longer. That day is
dead. The wind and rain, the ceaseless sun, the endless
days. The work, the dust, the drought. It's broken
now, this stone that praised a life. It's broken now.
The earth will break us all.

Ashes in the Wind (the Voices Rise)

for Ray Caballero

1917

A Poor Farm's not a place to raise a son.

No kind of place at all. But better than

the concrete of the street. And so they

sent me here—me—a city boy who thought

a stalk of corn was sugarcane. Where else

to go? And so I came. A Farm. For men like

me. I was down and down and out. My luck's

been rotten as my teeth. The fire took

my house and took my wife, and took my

first born, too. This place took me in—

a bed and food, a place to urinate and

crap. I'm not complainin' much. This farm

was sometimes kind. But it was mostly

cruel. The summer nights so hot, I thought

I'd sometimes drown in my own sweat—

'specially when it rained on August

nights. Could almost see the steam arisin'

from my skin like smoke from thirsty

forests caught on fire. For three years

this was home. What I learned in these

three ragged years? I learned to bend my

back as if it were a limb about to break.

I learned to hate. I learned to love. And one

November day, I thought I felt God's touch
in the cotton that I picked. I learned to pray.
I learned to bury tears like a dog would hide
a bone. And also learned to grow tomatoes
saints of God would sell their souls to taste.
Tomatoes! God! Red as dying summer suns.
I dreamed that red the night before I died.

1944

My father was a soldier. My mom, a prostitute.
At times, I lie awake and think of her and him
and how it was the night I came to be. I wonder
what she charged. I wonder if he bartered or
paid the price she asked. I'm not supposed to
know. But I could fill the county dump with
things I shouldn't know. (But what's the fuss?
No vein that flows with blood is free of
trash). It's not so bad to be an orphan on
this farm. They're kind to me. A hundred others
live the way I live, eat the food I eat, read
the books I read. Do the work I do. My heart's
not always full—but my stomach's never empty.
And on this piece of land I've grown tall as
stalks of corn in mid-July.

On winter nights, I've stood
out on the fields and seen a million stars

that burn with fires I'll never, never

know. But there are fires on this good earth

that burn with hate and rage. In Germany

and France. And Italy. Japan. The world's

ablaze. And me, I have some fires of my own.

Tomorrow, when I wake, I'll be of legal age.

A man. I'm off to war. I'm off to war.

1946

I heard the news today. Rejoicing in the

streets. A band is playing in the square.

We beat the Nazi dogs. We beat them down.

Japan is next. But something else I heard,

another bit of news. A boy who came to

us when he was five, a dark-skinned

boy whose eyes burned like the candles

in a church—that boy, the finest crop

we ever raised on this poor farm.

A man an hour. Now he's killed at war.

Is it a sin because I ask what for?

They told me not to cry. "Helen, he's

a hero. We raised an angel on this farm.

Imagine that!" I watched her move her lips

but kept my tongue. What sense is this,

to send a man to war? What sense is this,

to kill a man, then praise him like a God?

2000

To walk these corridors at dawn. To smell
the past as if it were the rising yeast
of bread. To walk these darkened halls of ash,
dust and rotted wood. Adobe melting
in the sun. To slowly turn. To hear the
footsteps of the past. You swear you hear those
steps. Through shattered windows, you can see
the crops. Ignore the broken glass. Look passed
the windows of this place. You want to reach
and taste the leaves. This old and trampled soil
can still bear fruit. The summer green you see
will bend the heart, then break it right in half.

Perhaps, this year, a harvest for the poor.
At last. This year. A harvest for the poor.

IV.

Notes from the City
in Which I Live

Notes from the City in Which I Live:
Poetry and the Political Imagination

---

for Bobby Byrd

I.

It is one of the great ironies of my life that I have turned to poetry to express my passions, my obsessions, my need to understand history and the culture I live in. I have turned to poetry to give a certain order to the chaos of my heart. I have turned to poetry to think, to pause, to meditate, and to express my bléssed rage for the politics that have shaped my life and the lives of countless others.

When all of this began, this early obsession with words and order, I had no idea where it would lead. But poetry was the beginning. When I was young and began to write poetry, I didn't give much thought to the meaning of words. Maybe young men are like that. Meaning did not matter. What mattered most to me was the rhythm, the sound, the mood, the aesthetic. I was concerned with creating beauty, though the very idea of beauty was something vague and ill formed. Vague as the idea was, beauty became my subject matter. That was what poetry was supposed to do—help you find the beautiful. Perhaps poetry itself was an essential part of the beautiful. Poetry represented something pure and ideal and untouchable. And it had to, *had to be* lyrical and graceful. And so I, who was clumsy and graceless, I who could not make language do what I wanted it to do, I who was not pure, gave up the writing of poetry.

Many years passed before I picked up writing poetry again. I set out to learn my craft and write precisely and master the language as best I could. I felt I had something to say and felt that I might have some talent (though I have always been suspicious of a word that masks more than it illuminates). I also felt that, to be a poet, I had to be completely and utterly in love with the whole idea of poetry. All other loves and passions had to be brushed aside like dead leaves or litter on the street or dust on the wood floors. Now, so many years later, it all sounds too simple and sincere. Too romantic and adolescent. And too impossible and demanding. I had too many other passions. And I was too greedy. There were too many attractions in the world that vied for my attentions. And I was not about to choose only one god—especially a god as jealous as poetry.

Slowly, I began to realize that the writing of poetry was a far more complicated business than I had ever thought—an art that was not nearly as pure as I had imagined or been told it was. I will confess that I was a full adult when I set out to write serious poetry, and I don't know what possessed me. I should've known better. But I didn't—and this is both my shame and what helped me to survive. I simply did not know any better. I probably had no right to be that naïve. But there it is.

In the beginning, I was completely taken with the process of learning to write a poem. I was learning a new language, and in learning any new language, it is inevitable that speech becomes tentative and simple—and resembles the speech of a child. At first I overstated or misstated. Next, I became a habitual over-writer like a child who was trying too hard. Though I was completely sincere in my desire to learn, I was unsophisticated when it came to poetic matters. Poetry was not a field I was proficient in. I'd read Shakespeare, Neruda, Lorca, Donne, T.S. Eliot, Dickinson, Wordsworth, Dante, Chaucer, Shelly, Whitman and Robert Frost. Good Catholic boy that I was, I'd also read the poems of Teresa of Avila, of San Juan de la Cruz, and many poems by Thomas Merton. And of course, I read the quintessential poet of the sixties, Kahlil Gibran. My reading of poetry was hardly systematic. I knew very little about contemporary American poetry though I had read some e.e. cummings and the "populist poet" Carl Sandburg. I had, of course, read Ginsberg's "Howl" with great interest. (On some days I liked that poem very much. On other days, I'd shake my head: "Enough already. ¡Basta! ¡Ya no chingues!") A few names were familiar—Levertov, Rich, William Carlos Williams, Pound. Perhaps I'd read a poem by these poets. I knew next to nothing.

I don't know exactly what drew me to poetry—especially since I was also drawn to writing fiction. Unlike the art of fiction, the art of poetry intimidated me. Poetry was a high art, a moral art, an art that "elevated the souls of men" or some such thing. That's what I'd been taught and anyone who'd ever read a poem out loud in a classroom in my day always did so as if they were invoking God or one of his saints or exorcising the demons in the world. It was a grave thing, the reading of poetry. Serious. I confess now that no poet presented to me in a classroom ever elevated my soul or any other part of me. In fact, I hated poetry. I suspect now that many teachers used poetry to remind their students that they had no taste or class or intelligence. Poetry was used as a cultural gun placed to our heads. Poetry shoved us even further toward exile and became a reminder that we were not worthy.

Perhaps, in the beginning, because of my Chicano Catholic upbringing and my theological training in the seminary, I brought to poetry a religious framework, a Catholic filter. I was comfortable with religious metaphors and allusions. Given my background, it wasn't surprising that, at first, I thought of poetry as some kind of sacred space, a confessional booth, a place where a sacrament took place, a place where I was cleansed if not forgiven, a place where I could see myself and the world more clearly. I also thought of poetry as a discipline. As a habit. It was not necessarily something you had to enjoy. You didn't go to mass because you felt like going. You went to Mass because it was a material sign of fidelity.

My early poems were almost always about childhood events, sometimes cast in a fictional setting. They were almost always preoccupied with my own personal biography. They were easy poems—too easy and sentimental and sanitized. I think I was interested in romanticizing my Chicano Catholic upbringing. I wasn't the first to make that poetic and rhetorical move. And certainly there are writers who are still trying to force us into that space—despite the fact that we don't fit. Not there.

My early poems were certainly a good example of the kind of poetry that critics like Marjorie Perloff and Harold Bloom are fond of attacking. (But then again, that kind of poetry is easy to attack. It's like attacking a Hallmark Card for being sentimental—there is no sport in it). None of the process I went through made me a very unique apprentice. I don't care to read my early poems and I rarely go back to them. There is little reason to do so. But I also honor those poems because they are photographs of a man who is learning to walk. Learning to see, to speak.

The one consistent thing in my journey to becoming a working poet is that I soon realized I had a tendency to politicize my own life—to politicize almost everything. I don't use the word "politicize" in a narrow sense. I mean that I place my subject matter in a broader cultural context. Everything exists in relation to something else, in relation to the polis.

Everything about me was created in a particular community. I was given a name. I was given a language. My identity was born out of a particular place and a particular people. My self-presentation was never merely about an internal conflict (though internal conflicts are certainly present). Even so, I can't claim my own conflicts are something that stand apart from the values and arguments of the greater culture around me and the community that gave those conflicts a specific face. Much of my work has to do with the self and the conflicts with the external world. I was never just at war with myself—I was at war with the world I lived in, *and that was my true subject.* But it wasn't just a war—it was also a love affair. Perhaps, it is more accurate to say, that one of my obsessions is my struggle to be connected to the world that invented me.

Recently, I have been thinking long and hard about the fact that almost everything in my life is political. I am enraged by our lack of respect for democracy. Ironically, the country I was born in taught me to be a true believer. And I believe in this democracy in the most radical of ways. If we believe that all people are equal, then it seems perfectly logical to me that we must construct a society with rules and laws that mirror that article of faith. All of this talk of democracy and society is to say that I have a fundamental basis for my politics.

I am not disturbed by words like "politics" and "community" and "struggle" and "social engagement." Unlike some poets and critics, I don't find politics to be a sign of corruption. I don't think politics has to make you narrowminded nor does it have to make you an ideologue. I don't think being a political animal necessarily makes your mind less sharp, nor do I believe that having a passion for the machinations of the world you live in disqualifies you from being a poet. I live in the world, a world that is cruel and heartless and unfair and unjust and beautiful and forgiving, a world that is at once chaotic and fragmented and harmonious and ordered, a world I want *to reject* and *to embrace* and *to change.* I know that in this one way, I am like everybody else who breathes and lives and thinks and feels. Like millions of other people in the world, I want to understand what it means to live. This is, after all, one of the reasons I write.

But there are forces that take us away from the political—ideas that seek to replace the very idea of "the political." But replace it with what? If I were to analyze the state of our culture by what is being published, then I would have to conclude that we are suffering from an acute state of shallowness. We are inundated with biographies of famous/talented/wealthy individuals of the present and the past—be they famous poets or famous entrepreneurs who name tall buildings after themselves. The memoir, the autobiography—this is the *genre de juer*. The privileging of the self, the aggrandizement of the individual—this is what our culture has become obsessed with—in politics and in Hollywood and in art and in *belles letres*. It is the personal that matters. The private. Memoirs and autobiographies become vehicles for writers who necessarily and inevitably become the heroes in their own narratives.

In the culture of the early twenty-first century, we manage to completely bypass the message (thus, bypassing this ugly thing we call politics) and arrive at the messenger. It doesn't matter whether you know or understand or believe what César Chávez fought for. All that matters is that you love him, now. You worship him. He is a hero. It is the messenger that matters. We reduce newscasters, politicians, writers, and even activists to the status of matinee idols. This aggrandizement of the "talented individual," this elevation of the personal becomes a rejection of the very idea of *the public* and a repudiation of *the republic* itself. We have become a culture that is obsessed with the self, in love with the idea of the supremacy of the unique and talented individual. We have become a culture that worships at the altar of the ideology of individualism. We have become a culture that is suspicious of government—at the very idea of government. This rejection of "the political" is itself a political move—but it is a political move that signals a retreat from the mud and the dirt and the uncertain and difficult arguments we must be engaged in if we are to be citizens of the world. The belief in "the personal" is a shallow politics of fear, a politics that pretends purity, that pretends virtue. This kind of politics imagines itself to be above politics while pretending to worship the human condition. It is the "individual" that is holy. All else is corrupting and insufferable. The individual is the source of all beauty; the source of what we refer to as "the imagination." Words like "community" and "politics" and "citizenship" only muddy up the clear waters.

Which brings me back to poetry. What is the purpose of poetry in a nation that demands that art be decorative and apolitical and removed from our historical and cultural circumstances? What is the function of poetry if we demand only that it concern itself with aesthetics? What can poetry mean if it is not socially engaged or does not acknowledge the community from which it arises? Harold Bloom claims that "mastery of metaphor and power of thinking are the true merits of the best American poetry of our time." I don't disagree with Mr. Bloom on this point. But I do find it strange that he makes this point as a warning against political poets. Mr. Bloom mocks the poetry of social engagement as if those who write it are sincere adolescents who are mentally and genetically incapable of entering into full adulthood. Apparently, he feels that you cannot possibly master metaphor nor are you capable of thought if you endeavor to write poetry that is politically engaged. I have heard voices like Mr. Bloom's all my life. His is the voice of an omnipotent misanthrope that I am—inexplicably—expected to admire. I have been warned and chastised over and over that the writing of political poems diminished *both my politics and my ability to write well.* But there is something else at work here. For some poets and critics, the writing of polit-ical poetry is an unforgivable transgression. "Forcing" one's politics into the sacred stanza is a desecration. Such an act shows a complete lack of respect for a genre that demands utmost respect. Political poets not only lack aes-thetic ambition, they have nothing but disdain for poetry. Complete and utter disdain.

 Poetry has integrity.

 Politics is dirty and unseemly.

 Poetry enhances your ability to think clearly and deeply.

 Politics is ugly.

 Poetry is beautiful.

 Politics pollutes your mind to the point that you lose your reason.

 Don't you dare soil the good name of poetry with your politics.

 Don't you fucking dare.

II.

 A few years ago, I attended a writer's conference that focused on the topic of "Community and the West." It was, as I remember it, a successful event—well-organized and well-attended with many thoughtful discussions on writing and how it was connected or disconnected to our lives, our cul-ture, our values. The entire event left the participants enough time to write and to think. As a workshop leader, I felt more or less useless. I often feel that way at such conferences. I suppose I'm ambivalent about poetry workshops—though I respect anyone who is struggling to write poetry in a world that feeds us violence, nostalgia, and thoughtless talking heads on a hundred channels on cable T.V.

One afternoon, there was a large session. All of the participants gathered, and there were well over a hundred people in the room. There, in that session, there appeared a rather large tear in the fabric of our fragile Western community. Because the discussion focused on the many communities in the West, there were bound to be differences of opinion. But as I sat in my chair and listened to some of the thoughtless musings coming from the audience, I began to feel myself shutting down. "I'm an engineer," a man behind me shouted, "I'm the only engineer here, I bet. I'm the only real minority in this room." No one on the panel had been claiming minority status at that point and no one was playing the role of victim. What the panelists were trying to address, as I recall, was the fact that we did not all view the American West with the same lens. But even this obvious and tame point seemed to threaten a good many people in the room. I wanted to turn around and ask that engineer where he learned to think. But what would that have done? For an instant, I felt completely decentered, lost, and I felt at that moment as if I were connected to nothing. I could not hear, did not want to hear. I could not be heard, could not speak. I felt shunned and felt, too, that I was shunning everyone around me. I felt a sudden paranoia that my presence was equally unbearable to the people who sat next to me. I felt as if I were living in a condition of exile.

I took a breath. The moment passed.

Sometimes, that moment comes back to me and I am filled with sadness.

When you are alone—and you speak—you expect no answer precisely because you are alone. When you are in a room with others—and you are speaking to them—you expect something that resembles a conversation (though I have been to too many meetings where people don't even bother to pretend to listen—they merely wait their turn in silence). Conversation. Dialogue. Human voices. What I experienced in that crowded room that Saturday afternoon was not a conversation. A room full of people waiting their turn. Waiting their turn to tell everyone what and why and how they were the authentic victim among us. The real thing. All of a sudden, panel and participants alike seemed to have been reduced to claiming victim status. I can still hear the engineer. But to engage in this kind of discourse is to deceive ourselves. This is what we're particularly good at in this country: picking a difficult topic for public discussion, and then, unable or unwilling to face the difficult task of confronting that difficult topic, we manage to completely evade the heart of the matter.

While it is true that we have separate identities, it does not follow that because we are individuals we are therefore an oppressed minority. It would be ridiculous if a university president got up and claimed minority status on the basis of the fact that he or she was the only university president on campus. We cannot ignore the positions we hold. We cannot pretend we are powerless when we are not. We all occupy different positions in this world and we all have different relations to institutions and power structures, and it is disingenuous to think that we occupy equal positions simply by claiming minority status on the basis of "being an individual." There *are* victims in our society—a fact that neither a political figure like George W. Bush nor a literary critic like Harold Bloom can erase, however uncomfortable it makes them.

There are victims in this country just as there are groups of people who have not been allowed full participation in our democracy. If we turn ourselves into nothing more than a collection of individuals, then we are all minorities, and—presto!—we have erased the material fact of discrimination. Though the rooms of the many panels and discussions I have participated in over the years seem to be full of people who have an overwhelming need to be heard, there does not seem to be an equally overwhelming need to listen. This is individualism at its fractured extreme. I refuse to glorify this kind of postmodern cacophony.

How did we arrive at this point? A partial answer lies in our ambivalent attitude to the concept of community. We are drunk on the mythology of the rugged individual. We love our personal freedoms, demand them, feel we are entitled to them, *feel we have earned them all by ourselves.* But we are not so enamored of the responsibilities that come with having those rights. There is no such thing as a civil society without civil rights. But there is also no such thing as a civil society in a country of adolescents who feel entitled to take but who feel no obligation to give. The city, the *polis*, has made a comfortable life possible. The city takes care of my trash, makes it possible for me to flush my own crap out of my house with a flick of the wrist, pays for a group of men and women to come to my house and put out a fire. And yet we absolutely detest the city. We live under the illusion that our lives would be more comfortable without government. The truth is our lives would be chaos without government and the services it provides us, its citizens.

There is another reason, I think, that we are ambivalent about the notion of community: the very nature of our history. We are both proud and ashamed of our immigrant past. The immigrants of the past (our parents and grandparents and great-grandparents) were good and virtuous and hardworking. The immigrants of the present are not quite so virtuous, not quite so good. Not quite so hardworking. And not quite so European.

We have a distorted and divided national consciousness about our own history. We have a great deal invested in our national myths—and we have a tendency to sanitize our past as if the building of the American empire was a bloodless and glorious enterprise. This manner of presenting our history is flat, uninteresting, untrue, and intellectually unchallenging. The kind of nationalistic discourse we promulgate is defensive, shallow and unworthy of thinking adults. A history museum director in the state of Texas explained, "We don't show the brutality of slavery because we do have groups of fourth graders, and do you want to show them a picture of a lynching?"

Most Americans simply cannot bear to hear that our national history is bitter, complicated and contested. We pretend that the building of this nation was not a political matter. We cannot bear to admit to ourselves that in order to build this nation we paid, *and made others pay with their backs and with their lives*. We all, *we* all have blood on our hands. We have built great cities and we have built a great nation. We are not an amoral people but neither are we that new and innocent nation we so like to think of ourselves as being. We have more than mastered Europe's penchant for conquering. We have killed, we have enslaved, we have committed genocide. When poets or historians or intellectuals or citizens who have suffered injustices and atrocities raise their voices and demand that our history be examined more rigorously, they are labeled as belonging to "a school of resenters." We have become incapable of coming to terms with the history that has quite literally given us the piece of ground on which we walk.

If an American Indian speaks painfully and angrily of the legacy of betrayal and the systematic extermination of the 500 nations that once ruled

103

North America, and if that American Indian speaks and writes in the traditions of his own people, then our response is, *well, all right, all right, but do you have to be so angry about it?* If a black woman speaks movingly not only about the past enslavement of her people, but of the present day obstacles she faces in order to become a fully enfranchised citizen, our response is a rolling of the eyes, a nodding of the head, *Yes, but let us get on with the more serious business. We are here to speak of writing.* We want to be forgiven without having to do the hard work of penance, without actually changing anything about the way we behave in the world. What is more, we do not forgive people who do not admire us—our culture, our ways of thinking, our traditions (however uncivil and violent some of those traditions may be). We are reluctant to grant other people's rage any legitimacy whatsoever. We want to believe their rage is simply a symptom of their psychological illness, a sign of their barbarism.

But all rage is not the same. And *I do believe that some forms of rage are a sign of barbarism.* The White Aryan Resistance, the Church of the Creator and the Fourth Reich Skinheads are all enraged. Angry white men who are angry because they feel that America belongs to them and *only to them* do not move me nor do I believe that their attitude should prevail in this democracy. It does not take a moral philosopher to perceive that Hitlerian rage at non-Aryans is morally repugnant. A rage that is interested only in the destruction of others, a rage that claims moral and cultural superiority over all other groups has no moral claim on men and women of good will, has no moral claim on the polis and does not deserve an audience.

But there are others who do have something to teach us with their rage. If we listen to the anger of the homeless who question our humanity by their presence—the rage of the man with AIDS who stands exiled from the land not only because of his disease, but because of whom he has loved; the disgust in the voices of women who have been abused, sexually or otherwise, by the very institutions responsible for their protection; the disturbed shouts of the multitudes left unemployed by our system of economics—if we listen to these voices, perhaps we will learn something about how to build a civilization worthy of the name. A society that includes only perfectly healthy specimens—physically, mentally, or emotionally—is a society that more closely resembles Hitler's vision of the world than it does an enlightened democracy.

In the early twenty-first century, community is suspect because we have an irrational fear that if we truly seek "community," we will have to surrender our individuality. Community becomes a monster that threatens to swallow up our precious individual biographies. This is the new politics. We pretend groups do not matter and that our association with groups is nominal and superficial and is as changeable as the clothes we wear. This happens not to be true. Our identities are bound up and invented by the greater cultures around us. To be sure, communities can be oppressive. If history has proved anything, it has proved that certain groups assert privileges for themselves and deny those same privileges to others. Communities can be small and mean and murderous. But the only real solution to critiquing and correcting oppressive communities is to form strong counter-communities. It is not acceptable to remain individual and fragmented and broken. A culture of individuals will bring us nothing but anarchy. It is unacceptable to retreat into the "private" and the "personal." Now is not a good time for running.

We must speak about our brokenness and our rage. To name an oppressor (even when the oppressor is us) is the necessary first stage of freedom. But, however tempting, we cannot remain fixated on the naming and denouncing of the oppressor. If we do so, we will become parodies of ourselves. We will remain adolescents forever angry at our heartless fathers. We will become lost children incapable of becoming adults. "Oppressor" is not a fixed category, but a role certain groups or individuals play—a role most of us have played to a lesser or greater degree. We can get rid of the role without having to get rid of each other. I believe part of belonging to a community means we must stop exiling each other. We must imagine a world without exile.

I was born in southern New Mexico. I was born to a Catholic, Mexican-American family. I had the same background as hundreds, thousands of others who shared my experience. It is accurate enough to say that I grew up in a fairly segregated society. Tell me again that groups do not matter. Tell me again that we are only individual. Mexicans and Gringos interacted, were even polite and respectful of each other. But they led their lives, and we led ours. It is a lie to pretend that we lived in a separate but equal society. In the time of my childhood, the only public institution that integrated and welcomed us was the Catholic Church. We shouldn't pretend that churches are merely spiritual entities when they play a social role in *integrating* peoples *into* the greater society just as they play a social role in *separating* people *out of* society. In all other public institutions, we were more or less treated like unwanted aliens. We survived because we belonged to a tight knit community of Mexican-American Catholics. To claim our Catholicism was not only an affirmation of religious faith—it was also a practical politics of survival. We belonged to each other and we belonged to the Church. It is incorrect to spiritualize our history (and equally incorrect to rob our history of its spirituality). My identity is bound up with the people who ensured my survival. It is a supreme act of ingratitude to pretend that I do not belong to this holy and stubborn people.

To live only as an individual is to live outside of a community. To live only as an individual is to live outside of history. To live only as an individual is to live in a state of permanent exile.

We must imagine a world without exile.

III.

I grew up hearing the praises of writers who had a deep sense of place and an unerring ear for the speech of common people. But that praise was reserved for writers from other parts of America—and not the America I lived and knew intimately. Frost, Faulkner, Steinbeck, Flannery O'Conner, Wallace Stegner—these were writers who'd claimed their space. Their sense of place and their good ear won them admirers, made them great, made them all the more astute in their observations about the American landscape.

I live and work and teach and write and think in El Paso, Texas. I live on a border. Some would say I live my life on the margins of my country. I would counter by saying (perhaps with a hint of irony and not without a hint of anger) that I live in the very heart of America. Because I live on the border, this very fact conjures up certain images in the popular North American imagination. In my many travels, people are often surprised to discover I live in El Paso, and are astounded to hear me say that I would live no where else. Most people do not conceive of El Paso as a cultural capital, as a place where art thrives, as a space where the human imagination can flourish. People are almost always astonished to discover that so many writers and artists either live or come from El Paso (Jose Antonio Burciaga, Arturo Islas, John Rechy, James Drake, Ricardo Sánchez, Luis Jimenez, Cormac McCarthy and Abraham Verghese, to name a few). I do not think I live in the middle of nowhere, and I do not think a desert is merely a place that is defined by the absence of rain or by the absence of an old growth pine forest or by the absence of culture or by the absence of coffee shops (that look more or less the same).

I do not believe that the residents of Austin or the residents of St. Louis or the residents of New Orleans or Los Angeles have a deeper insight into America. Nor do I believe they have a greater claim to American citizenship. I do not believe the residents of this city are parochial or insular or ignorant. We know far more about New York and San Francisco and Seattle and Miami than the residents of those cities know about us. We know America even when America does not know us. We know geography and the nuances of language well enough to understand that the border is not simply the end of civilization, but a frontier—the beginning of a *new* civilization. We know America, and perhaps understand the seductive beauty of its lies and its promise better than most. We know this country's language, its propensity for cruelty as well as its capacity to embrace and forgive and transcend itself. No one believes in America more than those of us who live and breathe and die on the border. And why shouldn't we know America better than most? Millions have died to come here.

The city in which I sit and write these words is a city that has been detested and trampled upon for centuries. Reporters and news people and various sorts of writers come and go and they make their inane reflections that are beyond vacuous, beyond insulting. They continue to create an image of the border that is almost always superficial and almost always racist. Reporters and other tourists love to come here and report back to the rest of the nation that we are poor—though they will never expose the reasons as to why this is so. These journalistic tourists will report that we are mostly Mexican and that we speak an English and a Spanish that offends the dignity of both Mexico and the United States. Time and CNN came to El Paso recently. They put together a panel. I did not attend. I have nothing to learn from these people and I, for one, am not grateful for that kind of attention. And yet their superficial representations that reduce us to caricatures are the least of the indignities that the people of my city have had to suffer.

If we are a poor city, it is because we have been kept poor. Poverty is not an indigenous plant that arises naturally from the ground. Poverty is a creation of human society, and El Paso—precisely because it is on the border—has been used as a place of cheap labor by American capitalists for generations. The labor of my people has been exploited for American profits and the benefit of the few. To add insult to injury, this country created an image of the lazy Mexican. No one I grew up with had the time to lean on a cactus. The creation of a racist aesthetic enrages me because I know that the *raison d'etre* of this aesthetic is to reinforce the myth of the superior white American who deserves to stand over the inferior brown Mexican. Racism informs much of the aesthetics and much of the history of the border. This matters to me. *This will always matter to me.* This history, this knowledge, this rage and this great sense of belonging affect my writing, affect my aesthetic, affect my grammar.

I once had a young woman come up to me after one of my readings simply to tell me to go back to Mexico. A fellow writer once whispered to another fellow writer that I was "an affirmative action poet." Another fellow writer wrote a note during one of my readings that I was "politically correct." I have had students and colleagues and strangers alike take me to task because I call myself a Chicano. I know better than to believe that people who attend poetry readings are more civilized than people who do not.

One of my colleagues once asked me what I was going to do once the border was out of vogue, out of fashion. Since when, I wondered, has the border been in vogue? Since when? I will always write about the border and I will do so because I continue to discover its depths, its incorruptible and stubborn humanity. I will continue to write about the border because the border is not merely a metaphor, because the border is not merely a literary trope. The border is a place. The border is my home. The border and its people are my heart, *my heart*, and I do not say that for rhetorical effect. How can I claim to be civilized if I do not value the people who gave me language? I refuse to believe that my writing is parochial or insular and insignificant to a broader discussion of American letters or American culture or American identity simply because I write from this place called the border.

IV.

It has taken me a lifetime to come to terms with the matters that tear at my heart and scratch at it like a hungry dog digging up an old bone that has refused to decompose. I understand that I am not, nor ever will be, a master of the language I write in. I also understand and accept that my many passions and loves are not as fragile or finite as I once thought. I value poetry and, if I did not, I would neither read it nor bother trying to write it. But I also value the world I live in and have come to understand that living in the world means to be involved in it. I remain a good Catholic in this one sense: I find it a holy and moving thing that a God would become a human being. This is what it means to be political—to care enough to become a part of the world. To embrace the world. I have no respect for people who stand apart from the struggles of the polis because they think themselves to be above such pedestrian matters.

I do not have to choose between poetry and politics and the life of the mind and the life of the body. My mind cannot type—but it can tell my hands to move, to type out words on a screen. And those words can become meaning, can even, at times, become a poem. My heart can only touch metaphorically. But my hands can touch literally. It is not base or shallow to touch literally nor is that literal touch necessarily unsubtle. I value my heart. I value my mind. I value my hands.

I have done many things in my life—and each of those things helped me to survive. I have roofed houses. I have picked cotton and onions and chile. I have worked as a janitor. I have washed dishes. I have served as a typist, a research assistant, a teaching assistant. I have delivered baked goods at five in the morning. I have sold donuts door to door. I have waited on tables. I have shelved books in libraries. I have known the beauty of work and I have also known how it can sand down a good body and a good mind.

I have held a tomato that I grew with my own hands.

I have had many passions and interests and choices. And yet, out of the many things I might or could have chosen, I was determined to become a poet. I don't say a good poet. I say a poet.

I wept the first time I held my poems that had become, *miraculously*, a book.

My life has been a narrow escape.

I was born in one of the poorest areas in the United States. My parents were seasonal farm workers. When they started having children, they moved on to less nomadic endeavors. I did not grow up in a middle-class household. I did not grow up surrounded by books. I did not grow up assuming I would become anything. From where I came, survival itself was success.

I did not grow up speaking English—though English has become my dominant language. I learned very early on that the world belonged to him who possessed the word. I was caught in the middle of a war between English and Spanish. Both of those tongues, I was constantly reminded, were on loan to me. My life was to be spent paying high interest on that loan.

The first thing a conqueror does is destroy the language of the conquered. Diego de Landa knew that lesson well when, in the name of God and the Spanish crown, he burned down the Mayan libraries. He erased the Mayan language and in so doing, he destroyed the Mayan past. The next time the people spoke, it would be in the tongue of the conqueror.

My education, like everybody else's, was anything but neutral. At school, we were educated *to* something. To be a part of something that was far larger than ourselves. We were taught to integrate ourselves into an American identity—an identity that loomed large and mythological and awesome. But we were also taught that the God we believed in was inferior. This is the lesson I took away from me when I graduated from high school in 1972: The American landscape was not my rightful inheritance. We, the poor and the Mexican and the Catholic, we the lovers of bloody saints and the pickers of cotton and onions, we who were the color of the earth, we who gave our hearts to the in-between and liminal landscape called the border, we were usurpers, visitors, ersatz Americans who were allowed in—reluctantly. Our assigned job was to be grateful *and to imitate.*

I was an average high school student who loved neighborhood basketball games and keg parties and believed in God because he created girls and the desert and mothers who made tamales that could make the spinning world come to a full stop. I was adamantly opposed to the Viet Nam war, I thought drugs compared favorably to most of the stuff our teachers were trying to force down our brains, and I believed that I lived in a violent country that was violent precisely because it had not lived up to its great claims of democracy and equality.

Even at sixteen I understood rage to be an important component of American life. Rage made perfect sense to me. It seemed an appropriate and logical and reasonable response. Why shouldn't Blacks and Chicanos be enraged? There was more than enough reason to be enraged.

In 1972, the year I entered college, I walked some neighborhoods

110

in Denver, Colorado on behalf of a presidential candidate named George McGovern. I was eighteen, and I had been given the vote. One woman on whose door I knocked told me George McGovern was a leftist that would take us all to hell. She offered me lemonade and a lecture. I left her house trying to figure out what she meant by the word *leftist*. But I had an idea that I wanted to be one. I think, at that moment, I began to realize the many shortcomings of my education. Well, there was nothing to be done except to go with my instincts. And so, that November, with my limited knowledge of the world, I cast my vote for Mr. McGovern. That night I watched a triumphant Richard Nixon on the television as he gave an acceptance speech to his almost exclusively white middle- and upper-class audience. I understood *right then* that, no matter how hard I worked, whatever my accomplishments, America would never belong to me in the same way that it belonged to those people who cheered on Mr. Nixon. *Not ever.* This knowledge has been a yoke I have carried. But it has also been my salvation.

I understand now that I had an advantage in coming to terms with the meaning of citizenship, a word that has always been harsh and holy on my lips. As a young man, I understood that learning about politics and the workings of public policy was essential to understanding my own life and my own place in American society. Which is another way of saying that I knew that my life depended on my relationship to my community. My Mexican-American community. My North American community. My life, my individual life made absolutely no sense without the context of community—a community that gave me identity and the words I used and the food I ate and the cars I drove and the music I listened to and the clothes I wore and the roads I took and the buildings I entered. My community that fed and nurtured me, that gave me life.

I am sad to say that I grew up in a violent and racist country. I came of age in an era of political assassinations and demonstrations, in an age of movements for equality by African-Americans and my own people. I saw with my own eyes the hateful resistance to those movements. I saw what happened in Chicago when Mayor Daley let loose his dogs of war on young people who were, in my opinion, sincere citizens who naively thought that this country was built on the freedom to dissent from prevailing views—prevailing views that had no moral claims on anyone with a good mind or a good conscience. I grew up knowing and understanding very clearly that democracy was something you had to fight for. I also grew up knowing and understanding very clearly that those in power believed they were entitled to hold that power. The possessors of the word refused to cede the world to the masses—despite the rhetoric of democracy.

But I also grew up in an age that gave me phrases like "The Great Society," "The War on Poverty," and "¡Sí, Se Puede!" and "I have a dream," and "El pueblo unido, jamás sera vencido!" I grew up with ideas like the common good and radical democracy and the redistribution of wealth and interventionist government that protected the rights of the poor and insured the future of a democracy worthy of that name. I don't hear those phrases or ideas from the possessors of the word these days. "Compassionate conservatism" is the phrase *de jeur*. It means, I think, exactly that: be compassionate to conservatives. Only a George W. Bush could make me yearn for the return of Lyndon Johnson. Say what you will about Mr. Johnson, and God knows my generation had plenty to say, that man passed the most progressive civil rights legislation this nation has ever known.

In all of this, I am not advocating for a return to the past. I have no use for nostalgia. Nostalgia makes for a nice evening with old friends over a decent glass of wine—but it makes for very bad public policy. *The future will not look like the past*. Nor should it. We must imagine a new future. Make no mistake about it, the past has been killing us and our people for hundreds and thousands of years. The inequitable, entitled, racist, American past. If public and regional historians want to wax eloquent about the myth of the American West and its greatness, then I have only this to say: the American West was built on the backs of dead Indians, and the slave labor of Mexicans. To praise that past is an insult to my people. We have in this city on the border a museum to the European Holocaust—yet we have no museum to the American Holocaust. We are not even brave enough to call what we did to the indigenous peoples *a Holocaust*. I am done with praising the past in the name of a false and shallow nationalism.

We have done our best to teach our children to be barbarians. We teach them to ignore the poor which is the same thing as telling them to ignore themselves. We teach them to pass standardized tests. We teach them to make invisible the two million people of Juárez. We teach them to forget their Spanish. We treat them as if they do not deserve to be full citizens, criticize them for the way they vote—then blame them for their lack of participation.

I am a writer. Somehow, by some great miracle, I have become a possessor of the word. I have learned, that through words, you can gain a small piece of the world. But I am first a citizen. It has taken me a long time to understand the meaning of that word. I belong to the people who have given me language, Spanish and English and holy, holy Spanglish. Rubén Darío once wrote: "Con los pobres del mundo quiero echar mi suerte." I am a son of that despised piece of ground we call the border. My fate lies with the people who gave me breath.

I have struggled with words and language all of my life. I have learned that language is used to dominate people. I have learned that every language is a way of translating the world and that no language translates the world without a particular bias. It is nearly impossible for me to attend to writers who do not understand the political nature of language. Like everything else, language is a weapon that can be used for ill or for good.

I have also learned that language is used by all people—and that no one needs anyone else's permission to use it. I have learned that language—like a communion wafer at Mass—is most alive when it is on the tongue of a believer. I have learned that the wrong word in a fragile moment can break a human heart. I have also learned that the right word at the right time can usher in an irrepeatable moment of joy. I don't believe in romanticizing the role of language in my life or in the world I live in just as I do not believe in romanticizing the role of poetry in the society I live in. I make no great claims for the poetry I write except to say that I continue my struggle with words and with language and sometimes I arrive at something that's at least worth the paper it's written on. Sometimes I arrive at something that is worthy of my community.

To say that I love what I do is no small thing.

In the end, I am the luckiest of men: I have fallen in love with my struggle to wed my politics to my art and to remind myself that *neither my politics nor my art can be separated from the community to which I am bound.* There is yet another irony in my life: I started my journey toward becoming a poet with the idea of the beautiful. I understand, now, what the beautiful

113

is. The beautiful is to be engaged in a struggle that matters. The beautiful is to be grateful for the ground that was given me.

This city on the border—this large and cruel and awesome and difficult place—this city has given me words. I return them to the city. This is what I do. I call this an aesthetic. I call this arriving at beauty. I call this poetry.

—*Benjamin Alire Sáenz. The Border. August, 2001.*

Notes on the Poems

The Rags of Time on Rio Vista Farm

Rio Vista Farm in the Lower Valley of El Paso County was founded as a "poor farm" at the beginning of the twentieth century for destitute people. It housed, for a time, families, orphans, and abandoned children who worked for their keep on the farm. During World War II, the farm housed Japanese prisoners of war. In yet one more transformation, it became an immigration processing center for the Bracero program for workers coming into the United States. The cover of this book was taken at Rio Vista Farm. The photograph is taken by James Drake who took many fine photographs of Rio Vista Farm in ruins.

The Word "Transvestite" Will Not Appear in this Poem

I owe the writing of this poem to the artist, James Drake. He was working on a project, documenting the lives of Juarez transvesitites, and asked me to write a poem in collaboation with his photographs. This poem appeared in its entirety in a book accompanying James Drake's photographs entitled "Que Linda La Brisa." La Brisa translates into "The Breeze" but it also refers to a transvestite bar in Juarez.

Work

This poem was specifically written at the request of the independent union in Juárez, Mexico (el F.A.T.) who in collaboration with the United Electrical Union in Pittsburgh opened a Workers' Rights Center in Juarez in 1997. I read the original version of this poem at the opening of the Center in both English and in Spanish.

After Spain: For Edwin Rolfe

Edwin Rolfe was born Saul Fishman in New York. A "red diaper baby," he was a fine poet who fought in the Spanish Civil War and wrote about it in a book of poems entitled *First Love and Other Poems*. He first published many of his poems in the *Daily Worker*, was politically active his entire life, was a friend of Charlie Chaplin, was involved with members of the Hollywood Ten and was hounded during the McCarthy era. He died in 1954. The epigraph is taken from the title poem, "First Love."

Elegy for Burciaga

The poet, essayist, artist and activist, José Antonio Burciaga was born in El Paso, Texas, but lived most of his adult life in California. He was an accomplished figure in the Chicano literary and art world. Among his many accomplishments, he was a founding member of "Culture Clash" and a gifted humorist. He had an uncanny ability to go back and forth between English and Spanish both in his work and in the way he spoke. This poem is a tribute not only to his politics but to his voice, to his style of writing—a voice and style that remains quintessentially Chicano.

The Stranger Goes Home (For Jimmy Baldwin)

All of the italicized portions of this poem, including the epigraph, come from Baldwin's famous work, *The Fire Next Time*. Baldwin, to my mind, was one of the finest essayists of the twentieth century. He was careful with words but never so careful as to edit out his passions and he wrote some of the most moving and powerful essays on racism in America.

Denise Levertov, Poet and Political Activist, Dies at 74

Levertov was not only a friend and mentor, but she was also responsible for the publication of my first book of poems, *Calendar of Dust*. The poem refers to her playing the piano, a passion she picked up later in life as well as gardening. She was a consummate namer and found it blasphemous not to know the names of the flowers and trees that surrounded her in nature.

She was in love with a heron that made its home in Lake Washington in Seattle. She moved there because she loved the rain—something she also needed to relieve her from lymphoma, the disease that eventually killed her. Seattle's weather also reminded her of native England, where she was born. She, more than anybody I ever encountered, had a complete faith in the power of poetry.

The Blue I Loved & Elegy Written on Blue Gravestone (To you the Archeaologist)

Both of these poems were written after I visited the old Smeltertown Cemetery. Smeltertown was torn down in the early seventies due to the fact that ASARCO (American Smelter and Refining Corporation) was spewing lead into the air from its towers. The Smelter is not currently in operation, but the black trailings of processed ore surround the area and have created a desert within a desert. The artist James Drake took many wonderful photographs of the cemetery and I wrote these two poems with his photographs in front of me.

At the Graves of the Twentieth Century

This series of poems is a shortened version of a series that I envisioned would become an entire book of poems. I may still write that book. *Deutchland, Deutchland, Uber Alles* refers to the Nazi National Anthem that has been outlawed in Germany. Recently, Fascist and Neo-Nazi groups in Germany have tried to resurrect the song in order to seduce people back into their movement.

Ashes in the Wind (The Voices Rise)

This poem, like "The Rags of Time" takes place on Rio Vista Farm, a place whose existence was unknown to me until Ray Caballero (the current mayor of El Paso to whom the poem is dedicated) took me there. Ray took me there to show me one of our historical treasures that remains, to this day, almost completely ignored. That it was used in a scene in the movie "Traffic" hardly constitutes the kind of attention this place deserves.

Notes from the City in Which I Live

I would like to thank Bobby Byrd for giving me the opportunity to write this esssay. I incorporated many of my unpublished writings to bring this essay into being. The quote from Ruben Darío: "Con los pobres del mundo quiero echar mi suerte" roughly translates into: "With the poor of the earth, I wish to cast my fate."